The 2011 Guide to Free or Nearly-Free e-Books

The 2011 Guide to Free or Nearly-Free e-Books

**Compiled for UKeiG by
Chris Armstrong
Information Automation Limited**

Published by the UK eInformation Group (UKeiG)

Printed by Lulu

ISBN (10) 1-870254-14-7
ISBN (13) 978-1-870254-14-4

Contents

Foreword

For many years in the 1980s and 1990s, UKOLUG published a series of guides and handbooks (as well as the proceedings of its conferences). Titles included the *Quick Guide to Online Commands,* which ran to several editions, the *Quick Guide to CD-ROM Networking,* and the *CD-ROM Practical Guide for Information Professionals.*

Over the years the Group's emphases and priorities changed and it became no longer relevant or practicable to continue this practice. With the advent of Lulu and similar 'self-publishing' services, publishing once again becomes viable for small organisations, and UKeiG has decided to resume its series of titles designed to assist information professionals in managing e-resources. This first title in the series, a directory, answers an often-expressed need at UKeiG e-book workshops: "How can we locate free e-books?" UKeiG hopes that you will find it useful.

If you have any ideas for, or would like to produce, a further title in this series, please let the management committee know at the following e-mail: admin@ukeig.org.uk.

Introduction

It is possible to trace e-book publishing back to the early days of the Gutenberg Project, when computer-based, archival copies of the Bible and the American Constitution were produced by re-typing the text in order to make them easily available to everyone. Consequently, *free* e-books were among the first e-books to be made available on the Web; today there are still free e-books available alongside the many hundreds of thousands of titles available at a price from publishers and aggregators. In more recent years, and usually in the context of journals and journal articles, the term 'open access' has come to be used as a synonym for free. It is defined as meaning that the "author(s) and/or copyright holder(s) grant to all users a free, irrevocable, worldwide, perpetual right of access to, and a license to copy, use, distribute, transmit and display the work publicly and to make and distribute derivative works, in any digital medium for any responsible purpose, subject to proper attribution of authorship, as well as the right to make small numbers of printed copies for their personal use" (Bethesda Statement on Open Access Publishing, 2003). Whilst there is a significant amount of free e-book content available on the Web, free or open access e-book publishing in the humanities and social sciences is reportedly increasing, and readers may find it useful to refer to the report, *Overview of Open Access Models for eBooks in the Humanities and Social Sciences,* from a project funded under the EU's *eContentplus* programme, which has looked at a variety of initiatives, and publishing models, business models and the publishing processes associated with them (Adema, 2010). For a longer discussion of free e-books, readers are referred to a chapter by Kate Price (2011).

It will become apparent as readers try out some of the e-book resources in this directory that a fairly broad interpretation of the word 'e-book' is assumed (if readers are interested, there is a lengthy exploration of possible definitions, and what the term means in an article I wrote for the *Journal of Library and Information Science* (Armstrong, 2008). In general terms it is taken to demand "a bounded and finished structure" – a phrase the City Sites e-book (*see*) uses. The important points so far as this *Guide* is concerned are that e-books are intended for reading on the screen (this does not preclude the printing out of occasional pages for reference, etc) and that they may derive from any source – being either scanned/digitised versions of print books or 'born-digital': e-books for which no print equivalent exists. Thus, users will find archives of scanned facsimile books, and single volumes or collections of screen-based, interactive works; there are e-books in PDF and HTML and there are virtual books whose virtual pages may be virtually turned; there is self-publishing and formalised publishing; there is experimentation and there is replication – some e-books look very like print books and others appear to be more like web sites; some even describe themselves as databases. Umberto Eco (2006) suggested in a virtual symposium that took place in 2001 that a book is the reader's "psychological mechanisms of attention" and Patrick Bazin wrote of the book as a "stable, reliable and public interface" between the author and the reader (Bazin, 1996, p.158). The essential fact is that these 'interfaces' can all be read, are familiarly book-like, and can all be read much as one would read a print-on-paper book. Some of course – specifically those that were created, and exist only, in the digital world – offer much more: multimedia and interaction, for example (as in Penguin's We Tell Stories), a possible departure from the conventional linear read (as in City Sites), or 'social reading' (Stein, 2010).

One of the problems which face all librarians adding e-books to their collections is that of bibliographic control: there is no legal deposit for e-books and consequently there is no single place from which new titles can be found. If this is true of commercially published e-books, it is most certainly also true of free e-books... and there are many thousands of free e-books available over the Internet, many of which are of a quality such that librarians might wish to have them in their collections. With my colleague, Ray Lonsdale, I have been running training sessions on developing collections of e-books in libraries for a dozen years or so, and it is no exaggeration to say that sourcing e-books is one of the most often articulated issues. We also know that many libraries welcome the availability of free e-books! (Interestingly, in October 2010, *Inside Higher Ed* reported that students were demanding access to more open textbooks (Kolowich, 2010) although according to another report they will not use them (Robinson, 2010)! See also (Hill, 2010).)

The 2011 Guide to Free or Nearly-Free e-Books is offered as a tool for librarians and others involved in book selection (e.g. teachers in schools) in all sectors – school, further and higher education, public and special libraries – to facilitate easy access to free e-books and e-book collections which can enhance their digital library. Whilst this volume does not set out to be an 'e-Books in Print' with title and author access (something which would be better made available online with direct links to titles), it does set out to facilitate that kind of access by pointing to secondary resources – one of which, the Digital Book Index, goes someway towards an 'e-Books in Print' resource. The *Guide* does list a number of single titles, in general this is where they are offered as stand-alone products rather than being a part of a collection.

Many of the descriptions in this guide mention formats in which an e-book may be downloaded or used and some of them may mention particular e-book readers. As a guide, **HTML** can be read using any browser and does not require you to download and then access the file – you are reading an e-book that resides on the publisher's server. This is also true of the various facsimile (or page-image) e-books. The remaining formats normally require downloading prior to use (and possible transfer to an e-book reader or other device). **PDF** files can be read using Adobe Acrobat or Acrobat Reader or equivalent on both PCs and Macs – the format is particularly ideal if you wish to print all or part of the book as, by providing a faithful representation of the printed page, this is what PDF files were originally designed for; it can also be read on iPhones. **ePub** is an open standard which focuses on the reading and is especially good with small screens – it can be read on a variety of e-book readers including the Sony Reader, Nook, BeBook, Bookeen, COOL-ER, Hanlin eReader, and the Hanvon as well as on the iPad and iPhone. **Mobipocket** or **Mobi** is one of the earlier e-book formats and can be used for readers such, the iRex Reader, Hanlin and BeBook and the Amazon Kindle, as well as on Mobile Phones and Mobile Devices including the Blackberry and Palm. Amazon purchased Mobi and developed the Mobi format into their proprietary format for the Kindle (**.amz**). Users of Apple devices, may like to know that in late 2010, BeamItDown Software announced their new iFlowReader application for books in the ePub format (https://www.iflowreader.com/), which does away with the need to turn pages.

There are good comparisons of e-book readers – including details of which format works with which readers in Wikipedia (n.d.) and in *ComputerWorld* (Grotta & Grotta, 2010).

Readers who wish to learn more about e-book publishing and use – particularly for and through libraries, and to keep up-to-date with the formal and informal literature are encouraged to use both the UKeiG Factsheets (e-Books and Social e-Books) available from the UKeiG website (http://www.ukeig.org.uk/factsheets) and the selective bibliography, *Writings about e-Books Publishing, 2010* (Armstrong, 2010). There are also links to similar selective bibliographies for earlier years. Users from the public library sector may also benefit from Ken

Chad's (n.d.) Local Government Library Technology review which includes e-book systems currently in use in its 'Systems used in Public Libraries' section.

I make no claims that all available free e-books can be found through this directory – it is not and could not be comprehensive, but it is a *Guide* to the best of what is currently available, listing all of the more important resources. It is a by-product of over ten years' work on the bibliographic control of e-books and on locating e-books on the Internet. Any reader who knows of significant free e-book resources that are missing from the collection is encouraged to let me know.

The directory is essentially descriptive, with some analysis of the merits (or otherwise) of particular sources. By and large, this directory does not offer literary or textual criticism although where particular issues have been identified, these are acknowledged.

Organisation of book
The directory is organised in two main sections. There is a slightly artificial distinction between adult and 'younger than adult' and, as a result, some of the resources are listed in both sections. For the much larger, adult section, the resources are divided up as follows:

> Archives and Collections
> Publishers
>> Mainstream Publishers
>> University Presses
>> Professional Bodies and Learned Society Publishers
>> Publisher Gateways
>> Self Publishing
> Single Titles
> Experimental Publishing
> Social e-Books
> Gateways
> Search Engines

There is also a 'Late entries' section followed by two indexes: a general index and a title index.

All links in this volume were validated in week beginning 3rd January 2011.

References

Adema, Janneke (2010) *Overview of Open Access Models for eBooks in the Humanities and Social Sciences.* EU: eContentplus.

Armstrong, Chris (2010) *Writings about e-Books Publishing, 2010.* Available at: http://www.i-a-l.co.uk/resource_ebook2010.html. [Earlier years also available.]

Armstrong, Chris (2008) Books in a virtual world: The evolution of the e-book and its lexicon. *Journal of Library and Information Science* 40 (3): 193-206. Available via the Aberystwyth University Institutional Repository at http://hdl.handle.net/2160/647.

Bazin, Patrick (1996) Towards Metareading. *In* Nunberg, Geoffrey (ed.) *The Future of the Book.* University of California Press. pp. 153-168.

Bethesda Statement on Open Access Publishing (2003). Available at: http://www.earlham.edu/~peters/fos/bethesda.htm.

Chad, Ken (n.d.) *Local Government Library Technology.* [Wiki] Available at: http://lglibtech.wikispaces.com/.

Eco, Umberto (2006) Discussion in Origgi, Gloria (ed.) *Text-E: text in the Age of the Internet.* London: Palgrave Macmillan. 288pp.

Grotta, Sally Wiener & Daniel Grotta (2010) E-reader roundup: 8 devices compete for the crown. *Computerworld* (14th September 2010). Available at: http://tinyurl.com/3xsdnlm.

Hill, Rebecca (2010) Turning the Page: Forget about those bulky backbreakers, digital textbooks are the future. *School Library Journal* (1st October 2010). Available at: http://tinyurl.com/2aduoc6.

Kolowich, Steve (2010) A Call for Open Textbooks. *Inside Higher Ed* (1st October 2010). Available at: http://www.insidehighered.com/news/2010/10/01/textbooks.

Price, Kate (2011) E-books for Free: Finding, creating, and managing freely available texts. *In:* Kate Price & Virginia Havergal (eds.) *E-Books in Libraries: A Practical Guide.* London: Facet.

Robinson, Sherry (2010) Students Use of an Online Textbook: Even if it's free, will they buy it? *Proceedings of the Allied Academies International Conference, Academy of Educational Leadership, New Orleans, LA, April 14-16, 2010.* 15 (1): 44-49. Available at (PDF): http://tinyurl.com/2vxxv4b.

Stein, Bob (2010) Proposing a Taxonomy of Social Reading. Available at: http://futureofthebook.org/social-reading/.

Wikipedia (n.d.) *Comparison of e-book readers.* Wikipedia. Available at: http://en.wikipedia.org/wiki/Comparison_of_e-book_readers#Supported_File_Formats.

Biographical Note

Chris Armstrong is Managing Director of Information Automation Limited (IAL), a consultancy, research and training company in the library and information management sector which was established in 1987. Chris's work focuses on electronic information resources, and their effective use in libraries and information centres. In recent years, e-books have been the subject of much of the company's research work, and it was a partner in the JISC National e-Book Observatory recently run by University College London. Chris and his colleague, Ray Lonsdale, jointly run a regular series of training courses on the management of e-book collections in libraries and Collection Development Policies for e-Resources, both for UKeiG as well as for other bodies such as the School Library Association, library authorities, and schools' library services. Collection Development Policies for e-resources was also the subject of a recent year-long project working with 30 librarians in sub-Saharan Africa, funded by the Carnegie Foundation, and continues to be the focus of a number of one-week workshops run each year in South Africa.

Chris has been associated with the Department of Information Studies in Aberystwyth University for over 30 years and has been Director of its International Graduate Summer School and module coordinator for courses on electronic publishing, as well as offering occasional lectures and short courses on e-books, e-resources and web-site design.

Chris publishes, and speaks at conferences regularly. He is a Fellow of the Institute of Analysts and Programmers (FIAP), as well as of CILIP (FCLIP), and recently spent six years as a CILIP Trustee. He has been associated with UKeiG for most of his professional life and spent many years on its management committee. He now works for the Group as part-time administrator.

Part 1: Descriptions: Adult e-Books

ARCHIVES AND COLLECTIONS

1. Alex Catalogue of Electronic Texts
Various humanities
http://infomotions.com/alex/

The front page of the site describes it as "a collection of public domain and open access documents with a focus on American and English literature as well as Western philosophy. Its purpose is to help facilitate a person's liberal arts education." The original, 1994 collection policy lists six criteria for inclusion. The texts must be public domain and freely distributed, and must be "great literature" (defined as literature withstanding the test of time and found in authoritative reference works) in one of three categories: American literature, English literature or Western philosophy. Only complete works will be collected, and whenever possible, collections of short stories or poetry will be included as they were originally published. The texts in the collection must be written in or translated into English as otherwise it would not be possible to evaluate or index them. There is also a stipulation over file formats: HTML is most preferred while texts in 'unalterable file formats, such as Adobe Acrobat' will not be included. No explanation is given.

Access is by browsing authors, tags (index terms) or titles, or via the simple search box. Browsing is divided into alphabetic pages so that it is possible to jump directly to any initial letter; and browsing by both authors and tags offers subsidiary lists of titles. Clicking on a selected title leads to a page headed by details of the e-book, including author, title, publisher and tags (some books have a considerable number). Details of versions (the URL of the original text and links to a mirror copy and a printable version) and the size, grade or age range, and the readability (Flesch) score are followed by a line of Google Ads and the text as a long scrollable, HTML page. Works are followed by a colophon which includes a persistent URL. Many – but by no means all – of the texts come from Project Gutenberg (*see*).

2.   American Memory
Various
http://memory.loc.gov/ammem/index.html

The Library of Congress American Memory project currently covers 18 topics, including Advertising, Architecture/Landscape, Culture/Folklife, Literature, and Women's History. Each topic leads to a number of collections, which may be searched individually or jointly. Many of the topics include e-books among collections of other resources such as photographs, songs and sound recordings; those containing books normally make this clear in the line of text following the title, although 'Multiformat' may hide some texts.

Selecting a collection (for example, The Nineteenth Century in Print) normally leads to a collection home page from which it possible to browse authors, titles and a subject index, as well as to search by keyword. Search allows multiple keywords to be input, with the options to use any or all or all as an exact phrase, to include word variants such as plurals, and to limit the search by fields such as title or subject; full-text search is also possible. Once selected from the results or browse list, the resource or book page offers summary information including title, author, publication date and medium, and a link to 'View this item' sometimes with an associated '[Rights and reproductions]' link which notes how the text may be used. Most e-books may be viewed either as facsimile pages or as plain text (HTML).

3.   American Museum of Natural History Darwin Manuscripts Project
See also: **Charles Darwin Online, Complete Works of** Manuscripts
http://darwin.amnh.org/

Subtitled 'A Scholarly Edition of Darwin's Scientific Archive', the web site (more or less hidden beneath a series of images taken from manuscript pages and the American Museum's other pages (Tickets, Calendar, Shop, etc) provides access to transcripts of manuscript pages from a range of sources including Cambridge University Library, Eton College Library, Harvard University and the Smithsonian Institution). The 'Darbase' is organised by collection, and access is hierarchical (four levels), each level refining the search from the source to the subsection. Search within any level in the hierarchy is also possible.

Clicking on a document opens a new browser tab – once again hiding the content off the screen beneath the images – containing a transcript, usually with detailed annotations, showing where an upper-case 'C' had been written over a lower-case 'c' or where several words are illegible, for example. Other pages are marked up to indicate manuscript emendations but no notes are provided. Each transcript pages has a link to 'View image' of the current page – this magnifies automatically as the mouse is moved over it.

Occasionally the link to the transcript results in "No xml data found".

4.   Asian Classics Input Project
Various
http://www.asianclassics.org/

Since 1988, the Asian Classics Input Project has been dedicated to locating, cataloging and digitally preserving the rapidly disappearing Tibetan and Sanskrit manuscripts that hold the philosophical, cultural and religious heritage of cultures dating back more than 2000 years. Founded by Geshe Michael Roach, the Project is currently undertaking preservation work in libraries, monasteries and Institutes throughout South Asia, Mongolia and Russia; specifically the current projects are Saving Yoga Wisdom; the South Asia Field Office; the St. Petersburg Catalog; and the Mongolia Project – the site describes all four projects in detail. Above all else the Project has an empowering and educational aim to work with Tibetan refugees.

There are five searchable collections, including Classical Indian Works Preserved in Tibetan Translation (Tengyur Collection, Derge Version) and Chone Drakpa Shedrup Rinpoche (Collected Works of a Buddhist Master). In addition, there is direct access to the Great Books of Yoga, Chone Drakpa Shedrup, the 8000 Verses Sutra, and the Sutra of the Fortunate Eon, with versions variously available as page images and in HTML or PDF. Some texts are available in English as well as in Sanskrit.

As this Project is in the early stages of providing Internet access to the many thousands of pages already digitised, not all apparently-available texts can be retrieved.

5.   Baen Free Library
Science fiction
http://www.baen.com/library/

The publisher, Baen Books is now making available for free a number of its titles – perhaps about 120 – in electronic format as the Baen Free Library. These books may be read online, downloaded in one of several formats (including HTML, RTF) or e-mailed to the user's Kindle. Download files are provided in both Zipped and un-Zipped versions. Often, where a series is involved, only the first two or three titles are available. Plot synopses and cover images are provided prior to access.

6.   Bartleby
Various
http://www.bartleby.com/

Subtitled "Great Books Online", Bartleby offers an extensive collection of titles divided into Reference, Verse, Fiction and Nonfiction. As an indication of the range available at the end of 2009, the service includes the 2008 *CIA World Factbook*; *Gray's Anatomy of the Human Body* (20th edition 1918); the complete 70 volumes of The Harvard Classics & Shelf of Fiction; the 1918 *The Elements of Style* by William Strunk, Jr.; the *King James Bible*; 1914 Oxford edition of the *Complete Works of William Shakespeare*. Poets features include Emily Dickinson; Walt Whitman; Robert Frost; William Wordsworth; T.S. Eliot; John Keats and Gerard Manley Hopkins. Fiction includes works by Fielding, Henry; Fitzgerald, F. Scott; Guy de Maupassant; Herman Melville; and Virginia Woolf.

The site notes that "The contents of the Service are intended for your personal, noncommercial use." The site is supported by 'Ads by Google' and sponsored links from shots.snap.com.

7.   Bartleby Reference
Reference
http://www.bartleby.com/reference/

In its reference section Bartleby (*see*) brings together a small, selective set of reference books in nine categories: General; Quotations; English Usage: Language, Style & Composition; Religion & Mythology; Literary History & Literature; Anatomy; Cooking; Etiquette; and Parliamentary Procedure & Government. The titles selected for inclusion under these headings are replications of the originals and are frequently not the latest editions – so, for example the 1918 20th edition *Gray's Anatomy* (the 40th British edition is the most recent) and the 2008 *CIA World Factbook* are available here, although the current edition of the latter is available online elsewhere (*see*). There is also a strong US bias and, for example the three titles under Parliamentary Procedures & Government, and the single titles under Cooking (Fannie Merritt Farmer's 1918. *The Boston Cooking-School Cook Book*) and Etiquette (Emily Post's 1922. *Etiquette*) are all US publications. In each case a full bibliographic record and the full text are made available, complete with indexes (e.g. the 10th edition of Bartlett's *Familiar Quotations* has a chronologic and alphabetic index of authors and a concordance index of quotations) and a search facility.

8.   BBC – Dr Who
      Science fiction
      http://www.bbc.co.uk/doctorwho/classic/ebooks/

The BBC has made available eight "rare and acclaimed" Dr Who novels as e-books. They may be read online or downloaded. Some, but not all, have to be read online on a page-by-page basis. All include, or have available alongside, the original artwork and author notes.

9.   The Bible Gateway
      Religion
      http://www.biblegateway.com/

The Bible Gateway is described as starting in 1993 as a project of Nick Hengeveld who was attending Calvin College in Grand Rapids, Michigan at the time. "In 1995 Nick became the first webmaster at Gospelcom.net, now Gospel.com. He brought the Bible Gateway with him, and for 13 years the Bible Gateway has been a favorite online resource. Today, the Bible Gateway team continues to add new translations, languages, and functionality to the site."

The front page of the site offers immediate access to the text of each version of the Bible via a search engine, while the full texts of the Bibles are available from the 'Available Versions' page. Altogether, just over 100 versions are available in 54 languages – about half are the New Testament only. Most copies are in HTML/text although some – normally the non Roman fonts – are available as PDF files, and some have audio files. Clicking on a version (for example the Wycliffe New Testament) takes users to a 'contents page' offering version and copyright information followed by direct access to individual books and chapters. Some versions are labeled as "For personal use only".

The site itself is available in English and Spanish, and pages are minimally supported by advertising. Pages have five font sizes available, and are also available as printer-friendly and mobile-friendly pages. There is also a page of reading plans to "walk you through the entire Bible over the course of a year". If your computer accepts cookies, it is possible to set a number of preferences (language, default version, etc) for return visits.

10.   Biodiversity Heritage Library
Various
http://www.biodiversitylibrary.org/

The Biodiversity Heritage Library (BHL) is the digitisation component of the *Encyclopedia of Life*, and is a consortium of major natural history museum libraries, botanical libraries, and research institutions organised to digitise, serve, and preserve the legacy literature of biodiversity. Contributing institutions are the American Museum of Natural History; The Field Museum; Harvard University Botany Libraries; Harvard University, Ernst Mayr Library of the Museum of Comparative Zoology; Marine Biological Laboratory and Woods Hole Oceanographic Institution Library; Missouri Botanical Garden; Natural History Museum, London; The New York Botanical Gardens (*see*); Royal Botanic Garden, Kew; and the Smithsonian Institution (*see*). The European Commission's eContent*Plus* program has also funded a BHL-Europe project, involving 28 institutions, to assemble the European language literature. In addition, negotiations are being pursued with the Chinese Academy of Sciences, the Atlas of Living Australia and Brazil to join the BHL consortium.

On entering the Library, users are confronted by a tag cloud of index terms which shows the relative frequency of popular terms such as 'Birds' or 'Evolution', but if this does not provide suitable access it is possible to browse by titles, authors, subjects, names, map or year and to limit by language and contributing institution. There is also a simple search in the first four categories and an advanced search facility. The collection includes over 41,000 titles in nearly 79,000 volumes.

On selecting a title Brief, Detailed, MARC, BibTeX, and EndNote citation information (plus a link to WorldCat to 'Find in a local library') is available as well as a link to 'View Book'. The book is displayed as a scrollable Adobe PDF file of page facsimiles, which can be alternated with the raw text. Curiously, while the link to raw text produces the equivalent text to the image being viewed, traveling in the reverse direction returns users to the first available page, often the cover. Owing to the header and menu bars above the facsimile, only half pages are visible and each page must be scrolled, although zooming (in and out) and viewing facing-pages is possible. The book may also be downloaded.

## 11.	Blake Archive
Literature
http://www.blakearchive.org/blake/

Visitors enter this extensive archive by way of a short description, which includes information on copyright, linking, citation and the re-use of archive materials. By accessing the Archive, you acknowledge that you have read and accepted these conditions. Fuller details – including editorial principles, a technical summary, a description of how to use the archive and a plan of the archive – can be accessed from the home page. The Plan notes that "In his lifetime, Blake produced about 175 copies of his 19 illuminated books. About 20% of those – 40 or so – have been reproduced, sometimes well, sometimes execrably, but in no coherent historical order. By the end of the first phase of our project, in June 2000, we had reproduced 41 copies, about half of which have never been reproduced before... By the end of 2003, the Archive contained approximately 4200 images, including at least one copy of every illuminated book and in many cases multiple copies, as well as a large number of Blake's paintings, drawings, engravings, manuscripts, and typographical works. A significant proportion of these will be fully tested and publicly available. Phase two will continue well beyond these three years, certainly." The online documentation is comprehensive and includes bibliographies, a biography by Denise Vultee with the Archive editors, a glossary by Alexander S. Gourlay, and a chronology.

Access to individual items in the archive is by means of the 'List of Works in the Archive' or through separate text and image searches for keywords, titles, etc. Image searches are restricted to a specific set of keywords which are provided in a series of tables and which may be used in any combination (all or any of the words ticked), while the text searching allows terms to be typed in and combined by the user. Text searches can be restricted to illuminated books.

The list of works is sub-divided into illuminated books, commercial book illustrations, separate prints and print series, drawings and paintings, and manuscripts and typographical works. Selecting a title – for example, 'Songs of Innocence and Experience' – takes you to a page with information on, and linking to, the editions in the archive; in turn this leads to an edition page with often quite extensive further information and lists of related works as well as a list of individual page images. The high-quality page images are presented using Java and can be resized to suit the user's preferences or needs. It is possible to move directly to the next or previous page, and there is also direct access to descriptions of the illustration or the text, the same page – for comparison – in the other editions, and to the indexes of object, copies or the archive.

12.   Bookboon
Textbooks
http://bookboon.com/uk/student

Bookboon is an online publisher of free e-books and in its student section offers free online textbooks. All e-books are available in Adobe PDF and can be downloaded from the web site directly without registration. They can also be downloaded directly from Facebook. To avoid questions with respect to copyright, Bookboon, which is owned and run by the Danish company Ventus Publishing ApS, states that "the textbooks are legal and written exclusively for Bookboon by academics from different European universities. The books are financed by a few in-book ads." The textbooks cover engineering, information technology and economy and finance, and can be located through the following subdivisions: Accounting; Biochemical Engineering; Biology; Calculus; Career; Chemical Engineering; Chemistry; Civil Engineering; Complex Function Theory; Economics; Electrical & Electronic Engineering; Energy & the Environment; Environmental; Engineering; Finance; HRM; IT; Management; Marketing; Mathematics; Mechanical engineering; Media; Nanotechnology; Organization; Petroleum, Gas & Oil;

Statistics; Strategy; and Study Abroad. Most sections contain about a dozen titles.

The author, ISBN, number of pages, a brief description and the full preface and table of contents are available on the web site, but although no registration is required and the web site states that you can download "without providing any personal details", it *is* necessary to enter the university at which you are studying or teaching, the course and an e-mail address before you can click on the download button. Textbooks, which are copyright jointly to their author and Ventus, may be read or printed but copy-and-paste has been disabled. The "in-book ads." are quite numerous and – in the textbook I examined – averaged one-third-page colour images, clearly labeled with invitations to "click the advert". Apart from these, the text and figures were clear.

13.   Book Glutton
Social reading
Various
http://www.bookglutton.com/

Book Glutton not only provides free access to a range of e-books, but offers a social reading experience too. Social reading can be described as reading and discussing the text as a group, and in the case of Book Glutton the group may be closed (defined by you and limited to friends, classmates or a seminar group) or open (anyone reading at the same time as you). Every page being read has two panes that can be opened to left and right: one allows annotation (either public or private) and the other offer a real-time conversation with fellow readers in a way that is not unlike Windows Messenger or Facebook conversations.

Initially BookGlutton offered a range of out-of-copyright texts but now they have added titles from McGraw-Hill, Spineless, Girlebooks, Hunter Publishing, The Disinformation Company, Random House, and – most recently – IT and computing books from O'Reilly. Many books remain freely available but some (typically those from the recognised publishers) now have a purchase charge before they can be read. The interface offers facsimile pages one-by-one centre-screen with the interactive panes on either side. Navigation is straightforward and there is an option to increase the font size.

14.   Books from the Past / Llyfrau O'r Gorffennol
Welsh, Out-of-print
http://www.booksfromthepast.org/

Accessible in either Welsh or English, the site from Culturenet Cymru provides access to a small number of titles which are no longer in print – the earliest from 1783 and the most recent from the 1930s. Titles range from *Caniadau*, a 1907 volume of poems by John Morris Jones to *Breuddwyd Pabydd wrth ei Ewyllys I & II*, a satirical political work by Emrys ap Iwan from the 1930s; and from the 1828 historical novel, *The Adventures and Vagaries of Twm Shon Catti* by T. J. Llewelyn Prichard to J. M. Staniforth's *Cartoons of the Welsh coal strike, April 1st to Sept. 1st, 1898.* A simple title list, complete with a cover illustration, author and publication data, and a one-sentence description, provides direct access to each e-book. Clicking on a title bring to view complete bibliographical details for both the original and the digital volume as well as links to browse the book as page images or text, to download the book in PDF, text (ASCII) or rich text format (RTF), and the table of contents and a search facility with the option to include Welsh mutations and/or diacritics (other search preferences can also be set).

Page images are approximately full size so that scrolling is required as there is no option to zoom in or out, but navigation within the book that allows users to move to a selected page, or the first, last, previous or next pages, is available at the top and bottom of each page. Clicking on 'Browse book as text' takes readers immediately to the equivalent text for the page being viewed.

15.   BookServer (Internet Archive)
Various
http://www.archive.org/bookserver

BookServer – like the Open Library (*see*), a project of the Internet Archive (*see*), offers "distributed vending and lending over the Internet" and describes itself as "a growing open architecture for vending and lending digital books over the Internet. Built on open catalog and open book formats, the BookServer model allows a wide network of publishers, booksellers, libraries, and even authors to make their catalogs of books available directly to readers through their laptops, phones, netbooks, or dedicated reading devices. BookServer facilitates pay transactions, borrowing books from libraries, and downloading free, publicly accessible books." BookServer aims to benefit authors who find wider distribution for their work; publishers that can distribute books directly to readers; book sellers who gain new and larger audiences for their products; e-book reader manufacturers that can offer access to millions of books instantly; libraries as they continue to loan books in the way that patrons expect; and readers who get universal access to all knowledge.

The only access to the e-books is by way of a simple search box to the Open Library / Internet Archive e-book catalogue, and entering a single term may find authors, publishers, titles or topics that match. The search results in a list of titles with author, publication date, publisher, provider, formats and language, with links to download the work in Adobe PDF or ePub formats. PDF versions are scrollable files of facsimile pages, which may be printed or have images and/or text copied-and-pasted.

16.   Bookyards
Various
http://www.bookyards.com/categories.html?type=books

Over 32,000 Adobe Acrobat (PDF) e-books in categories ranging from Art, Biography Memoirs and Canadiana, through Fiction to War & Military. Many sub-genres (for example, Art's 'Art History') are prefaced by an essay on the subject, found only if readers scroll down the page containing an initial, selected five titles rather than selecting the option to link to a further page to see *all* titles in the section. The site is lightly supported by advertisements, which only become intrusive in the essays where random words are underlined in green and linked to pop-up, but un-connected, advertisements. Each book is downloaded as a single file of unadorned text. There are French, German and Spanish titles in addition to English.

17.   Bored.com
Fiction
http://www.bored.com/ebooks/

Bored.com describes itself as "a place where you can find endless amounts of entertainment. We have free online games, fun sites, and so much more! We update new stuff all of the time, so come back often." There is no direct link to the e-book collection from the home page but the collection provides an alternative place to read most of the books found on Gutenberg

11

(*see*) as this is the source of most, if not all, of the books included. The site notes that an "eBook is similar (sic) to a printed book, the only difference is an eBook is digital. It can be read online and stored on your computer" (although there is no obvious way to do the latter).

Books are categorised in the left-hand column under headings such as: American Literature; British Literature New; British Literature Old; Music; Travel and Victoriana. Selecting one of these top-level headings produces a list of sub-categories in their place (from this point on capital letters are shunned in the menus); in turn, these produce a list of titles beside a narrow 'Ads by Google' box in the main (central) column, while the left-hand column returns to the original top-level categories; the right hand third of the screen being completely wasted in a bright red background with no content. Selecting a title results in the title list being replaced by the plain text – the wasted column and a lack of local formatting producing text lines which extend beyond the available width by one or two words, and thus run onto a second line. The entire text is read as a single, narrow, scrollable page.

The only title located that was not sourced from Gutenberg is the 2007 *CIA World Factbook* (*see*) which is presented only as a series of 47 textual representations of statistical tables (their introductions note "tab delimited" but this is not obvious) apparently intended for saving and using in a spreadsheet. None of the textual information from the *Factbook* is available.

18.   Botanicus
Various
http://www.botanicus.org/

Botanicus describes itself as an encyclopedia of or portal to digitised historic botanical literature from the Missouri Botanical Garden Library, and in fact contains some 863 titles (books and journals) in 3,821 volumes. The front page contains a tag cloud providing access by both year of publication and terms, but it is also possible to browse titles, authors and years, or by way of a map. There is a general and a taxonomic search facility.

Selecting any title produced a facsimile of the title page in the body of the screen with a floating toolbar and, in a narrow left-hand column, access to individual pages and a tool which automatically recognises and lists botanical names on the page being viewed. Above the image are 'About this title' and

'Download [size]' links as well as a drop-down menu of titles alphabetically adjacent to that being viewed. From the image it is possible to move directly to the first, previous, next or last pages, and the floating toolbar offers magnification, the ability to move the page around on the desktop (it is also possible to drag it with the mouse), or to rotate it clockwise or anti-clockwise, to refresh the image, or to download the page image at various magnifications. The image portion of the screen can be maximised at the expense of the left-hand column and the standard navigation to browse and search functions at the top of the page.

19.   British Library: Turning the Pages™
Antiquarian
http://www.bl.uk/onlinegallery/ttp/ttpbooks.html

The British Library's Turning the Pages™ provides access to facsimiles of a number of books from their collection. As the name implies, these may be viewed using software which turns virtual page by virtual page. The site notes that it "uses Adobe Shockwave, which can be downloaded free of charge. The volumes may not open if you block popups on your computer... We recommend you try our new improved version, Turning the Pages 2.0™, which runs on the Vista operating system (and on Windows XP with the .NET 3 framework). It will also run on other operating systems with Microsoft Silverlight, which can be downloaded free of charge... Finally, there are alternative versions that display static images (with enlargements and audio files) in standard web pages, in the same window. No plugins are necessary."

The works available for viewing are: the 15th-century Lisbon Hebrew Bible, the Baybars' Qur'an with "sumptuous Arabic calligraphy", an Ethiopian Bible commissioned by Emperor Iyasu around 1700, the *Sforza Hours*, Jane Austen's handwritten *History of England*, the first Atlas of Europe (Mercator, 1570s), the 15th-century Sherborne Missal, Elizabeth Blackwell's Herbal, William Blake's Notebook, the Lindisfarne Gospels, the *Diamond Sutra* printed in China in 868, selections from the Luttrell Psalter, the Golden Haggadah, Vesalius's 16th-century *De Humani Corporis Fabrica,* Sketches by Leonardo da Vinci, the original *Alice in Wonderland* by Lewis Carroll, and Mozart's musical diary.

Each volume is shown as a series of high-quality, colour double-page spreads, with pages 'turned' by dragging with the mouse and a 'magnifying glass' which can be moved over the pages and allows parts of the images to be examined more closely. The text, an audio commentary and help are available from within each volume.

20.   BuddhaNet's eBook Library
Religion
http://www.buddhanet.net/ebooks.htm

The Buddha Dharma Education Association's BuddhaNet offers copyright-free access to an extensive library of Buddhist works and teachings. PDF copies of each title can be downloaded for study. The works are divided into 'General Buddhism', 'Buddhist Meditation', 'Buddhist History and Art', 'Theravada Text and Teachings', 'Mahayana Text and Teachings' and 'Children's Books', some of which are illustrated. Some titles are available in languages other than English – for example *Good Questions, Good Answers* is available in English, Spanish, Arabic, Chinese and Sinhalese.

Each title is described briefly on the section page with a note of its size for downloading. In some cases a high-quality version designed for printing is also provided.

21.   Carlyle Letters Online
Volumes of letter
http://carlyleletters.dukejournals.org/

Subtitled 'A Victorian Cultural Reference', this digital archive from Duke University Press is based on the Duke-Edinburgh edition of *The Collected Letters of Thomas and Jane Welsh Carlyle,* both of whom were prodigious correspondents numbering many well-known names – Dickens, Browning, Longfellow, Darwin, Ruskin, etc. – amongst their friends and acquaintances. Both the printed edition and the online project are well documented on the web site. The home page notes that this is a live project and that further letters will be added periodically.

The archive can be browsed by date/volume, by recipient and by subject, and both simple and advanced search options are also available. The advanced search allows searching by any or all of: author, recipient, title, keywords and specific subjects; results may be limited by date range and there are two possible formats for examining the results. In the default, standard format with 10 results to the page, the display shows the total number of 'hits' and the search criteria, before briefly listing for each the recipient and the date written, the printed volume from which the letter is taken, and an extract of about four lines with the search term(s) highlighted. Each entry may be read directly or a number of items may be ticked before moving to downloading to the citation manager, which copies the citations to EndNote, ProCite, Reference Manager, Zotero, etc. software. The full text of each letter is provided on a single page with the search term(s) highlighted. In a column to the right of the text are listed the subject terms and the recipient, as well as links to similar letters, and options to have alerts sent as new volumes become available or to buy the printed volume. If you have registered (free) with the service, it is possible to save letters to 'My Carlyle Folder' for future reference.

22.   CELT: Corpus of Electronic Texts
Celtic Studies
http://www.ucc.ie/celt/index.html

The Corpus of Electronic Texts based at University College Cork brings the wealth of Irish literary and historical culture together as an archive through a searchable "textbase" of 13.6 million words, compiled from over 1,100 contemporary and historical documents. Coverage includes literature and the other arts. Irish, Latin, Anglo-Norman French, and English texts are accompanied by introductions, background information, graphics, translations where possible, and scholarly bibliographies. Access is by way of a listing of published texts or an experimental Google Custom Search.

The Table of Contents is also tabular, linking to specific areas on the page, but peculiarly listing six languages (plus 'Engl. translation') vertically with different columnar subdivisions in each line such as the language from which the document was translated, the century, or the broad subject area. The earliest works are in French from the 13th to 14th century, and subjects vary from hymnology to science and medicine. The structure means that it is not possible to move directly to, for example, a subject in French as the only subdivision on that line is century. Beneath the table of contents are listed all the texts in tabular format. For each entry there is a title, word count, and links to HTML, XML and SGML versions of the text. For some of the older texts there is also a link to 'Irish Script on Screen' where a range of facsimile manuscripts can be found (note that the link is not directly to the chosen document and that this is a separately hosted site.) Instructions for viewing XML or downloading SGML files are provided.

When viewing an HTML text the screen is divided such that the narrow left-and column offers a table of contents, which includes "Background Details and Bibliographic Information" and sometimes both the complete text and separate sections (poems, chapters, stories) while the main body of the screen is devoted to a scrollable version of the text.

23.   Charles Darwin Online, Complete Works of
See also: **American Museum of Natural History**
Darwin Manuscripts Project
Various
http://darwin-online.org.uk/

Available since 2002, the web site claims to contain "over 91,000 pages of searchable text and 209,000 electronic images, at least one exemplar of all known Darwin publications, reproduced to the highest scholarly standards, both as searchable text and electronic images of the originals. The majority of these have been edited and annotated for the first time with thousands of original editorial notes." It also provides access to "the largest collection of Darwin's private papers and manuscripts ever published: c. 20,000 items in c. 100,000 images, thanks primarily to the kind permission of Cambridge University Library."

There is separate access to the manuscripts and papers, and to the publications – which include the e-books and pamphlets, as well as articles, published manuscripts and supplementary works. The publications page lists titles as well as their contents. It is possible to link directly from the title to a page containing a description of the work and links to the sections, or to move down within the page to individual sections. Each section provides direct access to the text, page images and a PDF file and, if there are subsections (as in *The Zoology of the Voyage of H.M.S. Beagle*), it is possible to move directly to the text or images for those pages. Apart from browsing through this page, a variety of search options also exist – including the Freeman Bibliographical Database, and these are documented on the site.

Page images are displayed in a viewer which allows zooming in, fitting the image to the window, or to the *width* of the window, and access to the previous or next pages as well as directly to any given page via a drop-down menu. From here it also possible to switch to a text view or a text-and-image side-by-side view.

24.   Chinese Literature Classics
Various
http://www.chinapage.com/classic1.html

The site offers access to a range of classical Chinese literature in a range of language formats: English, Chinese text in gif files, PDF, BIG5 (Chinese text to be viewed with specialist Chinese software), and GB (Chinese text to be viewed with Chinese software able to read GB code). There are also some facsimile pages and photographs. The page offers a simple list of titles beginning with Yi Jing, the Writings of Confucius, Shi Jing (Book of Songs) and SunZi's Art of War and ending with the Classics Collections of Prose, History, Science, Novels, Classics, Literature and Poetry. In some cases, as with Confucius, the link is to a subsidiary page with a range of writings or versions available.

25.   Christian Classics Ethereal Library
Religion
http://www.ccel.org/index/subject.html

The homepage of the Christian Classics Ethereal Library states that it "seeks to build up the church by making classic Christian literature widely available and promoting its use for edification and study by interested Christians, seekers and scholars." The digital library is stored in Theological Markup Language, which is an XML application designed specifically for theological texts. Texts are converted automatically into other formats such as HTML or PDF.

The collection can be browsed by author, title, subject, language and format or via a tag cloud of popular terms. There is also a search engine with the capability to search within books, by title or author, definitions, scripture or tags. Advanced search allows Boolean searching of up to four terms (including author, publisher and LC Call Number) and limiting search results by language and format.

It is difficult to assess the size of the collection but authors range from Plotinus (c. 205-270) and Peter Abelard (1079-1142) to a T M Anderson who died in 1979, and titles include all 16 volumes of the *Catholic Encyclopedia,* Calvin's Commentaries, several dictionaries, several multi-volume histories, and 42 Bibles in various languages as well as numerous other titles. In all browse-pages titles are listed with symbols to indicate when a PDF version is available, and there is copyright information against some titles; in a search results pages there is an additional symbol to indicate that page images are available. These, like the version to be read online and the plain text version are free, while a small charge is made for the PDF files. Clicking on a title takes users to a page with a cover image, a brief description, a table of contents and access to the text in a variety of formats. Once in the text, users who are registered on the site may use the Java-based annotation and word definition facility; any user can use the Java-based help and next or previous page functions which are available in a toolbar at the base of the pages.

The site is supported by Ads by Google.

26.   ClassicAuthors
         Literature
         http://classicauthors.net/

The site is run by Great Literature Online and presents users with a simple list of just over 130 'classic' authors on the home page. Scrolling down to the end of the list reveals a section entitled 'What's Happening' (last updated in 2005) which notes that, "At Great Literature On-line, we are dedicated to adding free, HTML formatted e-text for your reading enjoyment. If you are a student, be sure to check out our links page for each author, especially if you are doing research." Authors in the list include Aeschylus and Austen; Carlyle and Conrad; Homer, Hope and Keats; Machiavelli and Milton; and Wells and Whitman – in short, many of the authors that can be found on most collections of out-of-copyright texts. The home page, and all successive pages, is supported by advertising in the narrow, right-hand column, which also offers 'Search' and 'Options'. Options allows the possibility of changing font size, family and colour, while Search produces two identical search boxes with no indication of any link between them: neither search box produced any results for title or author terms visible in the collection. Similarly the options had no effect on the design of the web site's pages, which remain uniformly blue text on white background surrounded by a pale blue border. Menus on other pages vary, some including 'Up' [or back one level], or 'Home' [the author home page, not the site's home page with its list of authors], or omitting the search option.

Clicking on one of these authors leads users to a page listing titles and titles online, a brief timeline showing varying amounts of detail and including when at least some of the books had been written, and a list of links to 'Resources on the Web'. Clicking on a title produces a table of contents/chapter list; from there individual chapters are presented as scrollable HTML pages with 'Previous' and 'Next' links at both the top and the bottom of the page. The default font used is Times and some readers may find the font size too small for easy reading.

27.   Classic Book Library
Fiction
http://classicbook.info/

** Site reported as unavailable January 2011 **

The Classic Book Library is a free online library "containing treasured classics for old and young alike." The Library is divided into seven collections: Historical Fiction; Romance; Children's Literature; History; Science Fiction; Science; and Mystery. The collections can be browsed from the Java-script menu at the top of every page. "From the menu, you can browse all books in any genre, go to the Table of Contents, or jump straight to any chapter. The chapters are divided into separate pages, making it easier for anyone to bookmark exactly where they were in each book!"

Books in each category are listed by title; a selected title is first shown as an HTML table of contents, and then as a series of short screen pages, with links to previous and next pages. At the top of each page is a bread-crumb trail, allowing easy access to the table of contents, the collection or the Library's home page, as well as a note of the page being read (Page x of xx).

There are over 150 titles included in the Library at the time of review, from such authors as Sir Arthur Conan Doyle, A A Milne, Jules Verne, H G Wells, Anne Bronte, Jane Austin, and Charles Dickens.

28.   Classic Bookshelf
Literature
http://www.classicbookshelf.com/library/

Just short of sixty notable authors are listed in the electronic library of Classic Bookshelf – these are a selection of the out-of-copyright texts found in many e-book collections although the inclusion of Sherwood Anderson, Kate Chopin, Gaston Leroux and Edmond Rostand is relatively unusual. There is also the possibility to search for title words. Also described as a 'reading program', one of the aims of the site is to demonstrate that reading from the screen need not be an unpleasant experience and the home page offers a direct link to one title in the site's Java Applet reader with the ability to change the appearance of the text being read. The site also offers users the chance to embed titles in their own web sites.

The editor notes that every month he compiles a list of the 100 most popular books – the last list, dates July 2003, lists *The Count of Monte Cristo* as top with 4.5% (of use?) and ends with Sherwood Anderson's *Winesburg, Ohio* (0.4%).

Selecting an author produces a list of available titles, while selecting a title offers a link to the Java reader or the chance to link chapter-by-chapter to plain text (HTML) versions. Both of these pages, as well as the plain text pages, are supported by advertising and links to Amazon. The reader, which opens as a new Java window, initially offers a series of options in the lower part of the screen with the text above them. When readers are satisfied with the choices, the options can be hidden so that the book uses the whole screen. The font can be changed (choices are: Dialog / SansSerif / Serif / Monospaced / DialogInput) and it is possible to read with justified or non-justified lines. Both font ('ink') colour and background ('paper') colour can be changed infinitely across the whole spectrum, and the font size ('height'), leading and margins can all be varied. Finally the 'Options' menu offers the choice of a chapter at which to begin reading. When closed, a single-line across the foot of the screen offers 'Close Book' and 'Show Options' as well as next and previous pages. The entire book is presented at once and reading moves continuously through chapters from page to page.

29.   Collected Works of Edgar Allan Poe
Literature
http://www.eapoe.org/works/index.htm

Maintained by the Edgar Allan Poe Society of Baltimore, the site brings together what is believed to be a substantially complete collection of Poe's works – poetry, fiction and non-fiction. The Society notes that "It is presumed that Poe's works, widely published for over 150 years, are part of the public domain and that no copyright laws have been violated in posting this material. Anyone is free to use information from this site for any legitimate purpose without charge as long as sources are properly noted."

The e-books are presented as HTML pages. Access to each volume or pamphlet is by way of a summary, leading to a contents page, which gives access to the individual tales or poems, as well as bibliographic details, a census of copies and a bibliography. Individual items (poems, stories) are also presented as HTML pages with original pagination noted in parenthesis in the text. The summaries have been produced by the Society and each gives a brief background; for example *Tales of the Folio Club* is introduced: "By 1832, Poe had published three volumes of poetry, none of which had succeeded in being the artistic or financial triumph he had hoped. With a touch of pragmatism, he turned from poetry to the writing of tales. Never one to merely dip his toe into even an unknown body of water, Poe plunged in with the full extent of his energy and imagination. The result was an ambitious plan for a collection of tales, designed around a fictional group of characters who called themselves the Folio Club. Although the proposed volume was never printed as a distinct collection, the individual tales appeared in the *Philadelphia Saturday Courier* and the *Southern Literary Messenger...*"

30.   Connexions (Rice University Press)
Textbooks/Courseware
http://cnx.org/

Like Massachusetts Institute of Technology, Rice University has taken the decision to make all courseware open access. While the site does not provide textbooks in the conventional sense, it does provide detailed resources for each module of each course available.

Darwin Online *see* **Charles Darwin Online, Complete Works of**

31. Digital Library of India
Various
http://www.dli.ernet.in/

The Digital Library of India's is part of the Universal Library, with the mission to "foster creativity and free access to all human knowledge [initially by creating] the Digital Library with a free-to-read, searchable collection of one million books, predominantly in Indian languages." Currently it contains e-books, e-journals and digitised manuscripts." Resources selected for scanning by the project are those which are out of copyright (Indian Copyright Act 1957).

The home page, which was re-designed during 2010, presents users with a search box; representative collections of e-books, e-journals, newspapers and manuscripts; author or title browsing; and the means of selecting date period (1850-), subject or language (Arabic, English, Bengali, Hindi, Sanskrit, Persian, Kannada, Marathi, Tamil, Telugu or Urdu).

Results are listed in short form with title, author and 'Other info' which includes subject term, language, publication year and length in pages. Clicking on the title brings up a longer bibliographic record including publisher and copyright information. There are also links to 'Read Online' and 'High Bandwidth Reader'. There is also a link to 'Admin Metadata' which gives further information, plus a security box to type in a word shown in the adjacent image before proceeding to the book – this did not appear to work.

The book pages, which open in a new browser tab, are available as facsimiles in GIF and TIFF, and in HTML and text (TXT) versions. Both HTML and text worked within the page structure and frame (with previous or next page navigation), but the TIFF version produced a new screen containing only the page image, with no visible navigation other than the browser's 'Back' button. GIF did not appear to work, possible as it may be necessary to download an 'Alternatiff' plugin or a plugin for Linux to read the books online. The 'Results' and 'Thumbnail' tabs did not appear to work. This review examined several (English-language) books and in some the optical character recognition had done a poor job; one bibliographic record (*The Works Of Charles Dickens Vol XI Part I*) led to the wrong book (*100 Years of Indian Forestry*).

32.   Early Canadiana Online
Various
http://canadiana.org/ECO

This English/French site has been developed by a national alliance of partners who are scholars and representatives of major research libraries from across Canada, as well as some champions of open access to Canadian heritage. Canadiana's mission statement notes that it "is vital to have a Canadian vision to present our cultural and scientific heritage in its bilingual and multicultural variety to our citizens and to the world, and to develop a comprehensive plan to provide Canadian Society with enduring digital access to that heritage." With this in mind their aim is to build open content in which there is "no requirement for the transfer of content ownership or rights; thus ensuring maximum public access within a framework of respect for copyright, including free and open access to public domain and public sector content". The content will reflect Canada's fundamental values such as bilingualism, multiculturalism, inclusiveness, and equity and promote internationally-recognised standards and best practices.

There are seven online collections totalling three million pages of Canada's print heritage published from the time of the first European settlers to the first two decades of the 20th Century. Early Canadiana Online (ECO) is a pilot project. It is important to note that ECO contains non-book resources as well as digitised books, and there is no way of limiting the results of a search to e-books alone.

The home page provides an advanced search which allows searching of terms in the full text, title, author, subject, publisher, collection, notes, all metadata, or document text only using all terms, any of the terms, the exact phrase or terms 'in close proximity'. Results can be limited by language and/or time period. It is also possible to browse through the titles, authors, subjects, publishers and collections starting at any given letter. The collections listed are: Colonial Government Journals, English Canadian Literature, Government Publications, Governor General, Health and Medicine, History of French Canada, Jesuit Relations, Native Studies, Periodicals, Reconstituted Debates,

The Fur Trade and the Hudson's Bay Company, and Women's History.

Brief records for each document include details of title, principal author and imprint, and subject terms, and direct access to the facsimile title page, and thus to subsequent pages. Authors and subject terms are linked to related works. Clicking on the title produces a more detailed record including notes, document source, and collection. From here it is possible to move directly to the title page or any successive page.

Pages are facsimiles of the original – sometimes of fiches of the originals – and may be resized, rotated or bookmarked, as well as downloaded as PDF files. It is possible to move directly to any page (pages which are illustrations are so marked) and there are tabs across the top of the screen to return to the search results, browse list or the detailed record for the document in question.

33.   eBooks@Adelaide
Various
http://ebooks.adelaide.edu.au/

The University of Adelaide's collection of classic works of literature, philosophy, science, history and exploration and travel states on the home page that it does not include textbooks or books which are still in copyright. From the home page it is possible to browse by author, title or broad subject area, and perform a Google Custom Search across the full content of all books.
From the title list it is immediately obvious that three versions of each title are available: an ePub version, a paginated HTML version for reading from the screen, and one complete, un-paginated, HTML text for printing.

It is important to note, as it may limit use to reading for pleasure rather than for study, that the e-books are published here as *new* editions and are not copies of previous editions – indeed sometimes, they have been created from multiple print editions. This means that no attempt has been made to retain the pagination or textual layout and references of the source edition. The FAQ notes that accessibility and readability have been the primary aim, and that "pagination is an artifact of the printed medium – a work is divided into pages simply because they are the units of publication in a paper format. With web editions, the unit of publication is the web page, which may be a complete chapter, section or even the entire work." Where the original edition is known, it will be noted on the title verso page.

Although there is no formal link, most of the e-books@Adelaide are created from plain-text versions available from Project Gutenberg (*see*) or from other free public-domain sources.

34. eReader.com
Various
http://www.ereader.com/servlet/mw?t=freebooks&si=59

Free e-books are only a part of the larger Barnes & Noble eReader site from which many other titles may be purchased. In fact, when visited in early 2010 only some 39 free e-books were available – many of these link to other titles by the same author which can be purchased, sometimes for as little as a couple of dollars. Clicking on a title leads to a page containing a description, a file size, category, publisher, the author's other titles, and the possibility of reading an excerpt. From all pages it is possible to add the title to a wish list or – even if users only wish to acquire a free e-book – to add titles to a shopping basket. It is then necessary to set up an account in order to 'retrieve' the book. Some titles (e.g. Conan Doyle's *A Study in Scarlet, Andersen's Fairy Tales,* Jane Austin's *Emma*) have a standard brown cover with the word 'Classic' and are made available from Barnes & Noble's other e-book site: FictionWise (see).

35. ESP (Electronic Scholarly Publishing)
Classical Genetics
http://www.esp.org/books/

ESP offers electronic publication of scientific and other scholarly materials, particularly the history of science, genetics, computational biology, and genome research. The ultimate goal was given as the provision of tools for electronic scholarly publications, so that others may also undertake projects at the site. The parent site also contains papers, but the URL given here is limited to books; navigation on the site is quite elementary (it is difficult to return from the 'About' section, and there is no obvious way to navigate to the papers), but the book collection can be browsed by author, title or publication date – in each case with or without notes for each title.

Although the site does not appear to have been updated since 2003, it contains HTML or PDF titles from 350 BC (Aristotle: On the Generation of Animals) to 1969 (a chapter by F. A. E. Crew: Recollections of the early days of the genetical society. *In* John Jinks (ed.), *The Genetical Society - The First Fifty Years*, Edinburgh: Oliver and Boyd, pp. 9-15). In all there are around 40 e-books, including works by Bacon, Darwin, Melville and Voltaire.

36.   ETANA: Electronic Texts and Ancient Near Eastern Archives
Near Eastern Studies
http://www.etana.org/

ETANA is "envisioned to include the permanent archiving, dissemination and generation of both front- and back-end stages of scholarly knowledge (such as archaeological excavation reports, editions of ancient and modern texts, core early monographs, dictionaries, journals, and reports in the public domain), ... [as well as] eventually an electronic publishing effort for "born digital" publications." It is digitising texts relating to ancient Near Eastern studies that have been selected as valuable for teaching and/or research. Primarily editions that are out of copyright, or for which copyright permission has been obtained are used.

In addition to some 368 core texts made available in PDF, the site also acts as a subject gateway to over 2,000 e-books available via the Internet Archive (*see*) and from other institutions. Both collections can be browsed by title or author lists which link to bibliographic records or directly to the text or e-book.

37.   Evangelical Library
Handbooks
http://www.elebooks.org.uk/index.asp
http://www.evangelical-library.org.uk/e-books/ *(new URL: site under development)*

This is the e-books project of the Evangelical Library, now based in North London – which runs a web site where can be accessed "the Library's growing electronic catalogue of the best Evangelical Christian writings around!" The e-books project seeks "to make this wisdom accessible for Christians world wide in a way that allows rapid discovery of the relevant sections of the text on the one hand and a full preservation of the original document in image format on the other." Only a few sample texts are available free – the remainder of the library requires a small

26

(UK £25) subscription, payable by credit card. As of early 2010, some 33 books can be listed in either title or author sequence; two titles are also available as page images.

38.   Feedbooks
        Various
        http://www.feedbooks.com/

Feedbooks offers a publishing service, as well as "thousands of public domain books and original books from new authors that you can read on any mobile device" thus books are either public domain or original. Many, but not all, of the public domain works come from Project Gutenberg (see). Books are given descriptive tags, titles by the same author are linked, and each book page contains a few similar titles (although quite how *War and Peace* and *The Adventures of Sherlock Holmes* are similar to the *Kama Sutra*, I do not know!); also on the individual book pages, readers can label books as favourites or leave comments. Titles can be downloaded as ePub, Mobipocket/Kindle, PDF or Custom PDF.

The 'About Us' page notes: "As a service, Feedbooks is a unique solution for e-books: it provides an easy way to find, publish and distribute e-books in a large number of formats, while focusing on creating the best experience for e-books... Our team developed its own technology to generate e-books on the fly. Using both semantic and presentation elements, Feedbooks can generate high-quality e-books in any format."

39.   Fiction.us
        Fiction
        http://www.fiction.us/

At first sight Fiction.us appears to offer an eclectic, alphabetic list of about 300 novel titles on a dark brown background, but closer inspection of the left hand column (the right is given over to Ads by Google) reveals further pages for Short Stories, Children's Picture Books, Plays, Books on Writing, and Poetry, as well as links to '100 Best English Novels', '1900-1909 Bestsellers' and '1910-1923 Bestsellers', although not all of the titles in the last three are available online. There is also a link to a sister-site Ideology.us (*see*). The various sectional pages are presented in slightly differing styles but in each case link directly to the titles listed, in some case by way of a chapter list.

Although all pages leading to the chapter text are supported by advertising, the text is presented as HTML pages: dark blue or black chapter text is on a clean white background, with a link back to the table of contents/chapter list at the top of the page but no direct link to the following chapter at the foot. Short stories, the four plays and the four books on writing are similarly presented, but the poems are each framed beneath further advertisements. The exceptions to the standard layout are the children's picture books. These are eight books by Beatrix Potter and include the original illustrations within the text.

40.   FictionWise
Fiction
http://www.fictionwise.com/ebooks/freebooks.htm

Like eReader.com, FictionWise is a Barnes & Noble company, and in a similar way, the free e-books are only one part of the site. FictionWise is described as "the top independent eBook seller in the world with tens of thousands of satisfied customers. We offer award-winning eBooks for all PDAs and PCs by top authors! Palm, PocketPC, Hiebook, eBookMan, Adobe, MS Reader, and WinCE eBooks. All new eBooks discounted each week!" Free e-books can be browsed by category and format, and sorted by author, title, etc. The resulting list shows a cover image, a short description and graphic "Reader Ratings": Great, Good, OK and Poor. Individual title pages show the same information with a slightly longer description and an excerpt from the book. Titles may be added to a Wish List or a Shopping Cart although, as with eReader.com, it is necessary to set up an account. As is to be expected, there is an overlap with content also found on eReader.com.

41.   Flat World Knowledge
Textbooks/Courseware
http://www.flatworldknowledge.com/

This US site provides a number of options, including print-on-demand for bookstores, but offers free e-textbooks to students whose tutor has 'adopted' the book for his or her course. Tutors may select books from a small but growing catalogue of titles in business and economics, humanities and social sciences, science, professional and applied sciences, and mathematics. Textbooks may also be customised. The textbook is only free to read on the screen but offers the ability to print chapters for a small fee as well as to purchase the complete book. Tutors who adopt a book – which may also provide them with instructor manuals, test questions, lecture slides, and solutions manuals – are provided with a unique URL to pass on to their students and an ISBN to enable their bookshop to sell the title. Textbooks can also be purchased printed in monochrome or colour. The publishers note that their model, offering students free online books with the option to purchase affordable print versions, still provides sufficient revenue.

42. Free e-Book Library on Yudu
Literature
http://www.yudu.com/library/42149/e-Books-s-Library

Yudu, the site for self-publishing of digital magazines, has 108 free e-books, including the 45 titles in the William Shakespeare's Library (*see*). Titles included appear to be the usual out-of-copyright editions (*A Journey to the Centre of the Earth, Andersen's Fairy Tales, Little Women, Madam Bovary, Mansfield Park,* etc) and all appear here in identical 'bindings'.

Hovering over a cover in the library bookshelves reveals the beginning of the brief publisher's description of the work that can be read in full on the subsequent page, which also offers the facility to embed the work in your own web site and to view the work. After a brief pause while the work is loaded in Adobe Flash, a facsimile book is presented. Having entered a book, there is no clear way (other than the browser's back button) to return to the library.

On a page facing the front cover of each book is a link to instructions for use, and along the top of the screen, over the book pages, are a number of tools; page turning is induced – with a slight rustle of paper – by clicking on the lower corner of each page. The available tools include the possibility to move to next/previous, first/last or any numbered page (there is no indication of how many pages make up the book) as well as print (with a choice of page range), bookmark in several colours, add notes or highlights to the current page and change to a "plain text" (i.e. in HTML rather than the facsimile) version. Pages can be magnified or set to fill the existing screen width and there are menus allowing readers to share the book (e.g. Del.icio.us), view thumbnails of all pages in a left-hand column or of only those pages with highlighting/notes, and of options which include downloading an offline version, setting preferences, viewing in single-page mode, and auto-presenting with a page-turn at designated intervals.

43.　　Free-ebooks.net
Various
http://www.free-ebooks.net/

Free-ebooks.net offers access to e-books in 45 categories, including Advertising, Beauty & Fashion, Body & Spirit, Fiction, General non-Fiction, Marketing, Real estate, Short stories, and Youth. There is a search engine for title words and authors, the results from which take readers directly to the HTML version of the e-book. Ranged to the left are other formats, Google translation, font-size adjustment, printing, rating and reviewing capabilities. It is noted that, unlike the PDF version, the HTML edition "may not be properly formatted."

Books can also be browsed by category or by author, and each listing – which can be sorted by title, rating or hits – provides a brief synopsis of each title, the number of times it has been downloaded or added to user libraries, and – possibly – a rating by other users or a user review. Once users have joined Free-ebooks, titles can be added to personal libraries.

Membership is required before you can download a book: without membership unlimited HTML e-books are available, but standard membership allows five PDF e-books per month in addition, while 'VIP Membership' is required before you can download books in either Mobipocket or ePub formats. VIP membership costs just under US$20 per year, and also offers "Store & Save: 'My Digital Library' lets you save your 'Favorite' ebooks & store copies on our server so you can always have them available - anytime, anywhere you have Internet access."

In addition to free e-books the site makes available an extensive list of free Business, Computer, Engineering and Trade magazines, white papers, and downloads for users "to find the titles that best match your skills and interests; topics include management, marketing, operations, sales, and technology." It is necessary to complete an application form and these are then delivered free to "professionals who qualify." The page is powered by TradePub.com. Free-ebooks.net will also publish e-books that are submitted to the site. The site is sponsored by Google Ads.

44. Froebel Archive Digital Collection
See also: Roehampton University Children's Literature Collection
Scholarly, Children's literature
http://core.roehampton.ac.uk/digital/froebelindex.htm

Roehampton University have made available the Froebel Archive, which supports courses offered within the university presenting comparative views of early childhood philosophies. Some 35 heavily-used books (many, but not all, by Friedrich Froebel) and eight book extracts from the Archive have now been digitised for use by students and other interested readers.

A simple author/title list leads to extended contents pages, which in turn link to PDF extracts, each usually containing four pages.

45. FullBooks.com
Various
http://www.fullbooks.com/

FullBooks.com – "Thousands of Full-Text Free Books" – offers a minimalist front page with links from "A-Ago" and "Agr-And" to "Zib-Zul" as well as what turn out to be links to remote sites with titles in Business, Nations and Countries, How Products are Made, Science, Films, Children's Health, Surgery, Mental Disorders, and Illnesses. Clicking on an alphabetic group lead users to a simple, unembellished title list; clicking on a title produces a title page offering access to unexplained book parts which do not necessarily match chapters in the Contents. The text of each part is sponsored by Google Ads so that users must scroll down to the HTML text.

As may be imagined from the granularity of the front-page alphabetic groups, the site contains a good number of titles: there are 55 groups and each contains an average of 150 e-books (much of Pun-Que is taken up by seemingly random volumes and issues (without illustrations) of *Punch, Or The London Charivari*). There is no other means of access so that all titles by any author may be spread around the site's 55 pages. Dickens, Marlow, Shakespeare, Shaw, Thackeray and Twain, can all be discovered as can The Bible, Bhagavad-Gita and The Koran, but there is no explanation of provenance or choice on the site: the e-books appear to be out-of-copyright editions – the most recent text discovered came from 1911.

46.   Get Free eBooks (*or* getfreeebooks)
Various
http://www.getfreeebooks.com/

Getfreeebooks describes itself as "a free ebooks site where you can download free books totally free" and goes on to note that the "ebooks which you find within this site are collected from all over the net or either [sic] personally compiled by me. If you think there are ebooks which you think that should be in this site, do let me know, or if you have your own free ebook, drop me an email and I'll put them up right away." Slightly worryingly, although claiming that all of the available e-books are legally downloadable a note of doubt is introduced: "If you're the owner / author of any of the ebooks listed within this site and wish them to be removed, do let me know and I'll remove it immediately."

The site appears to be a Blog, sponsored by Google Ads, with each title entered as a separate posting and tagged as e.g. fiction, family & kids, Internet marketing. There is a tag cloud of categories visible on all pages. As is hinted in the overview above, the e-books are described here but accessed from remote sites – including the self-publishing site, Lulu. Each posting includes a cover images, title/author information, a short synopsis, number of pages and a list of the formats in which it is available. Each also carries a warning that although the e-book was free at the time of posting it may no longer be so, and a request to notify the site owner if the status has changed. This appears to confirm a statement on the 'About' page that once added, links are not monitored. As this site is a Blog, each entry is dated and some have comments from readers; there is an RSS feed so that users may receive alerts of newly added titles.

Like Free-ebooks.net, there is a TradePub.com page of free Business, Computer, Engineering and Trade magazines to which users may subscribe in order to receive free print copies.

47.   Glasgow Digital Library Ebooks
Monographs on Scotland
http://gdl.cdlr.strath.ac.uk/gdlebooks.html

The Glasgow Digital Library open-access e-book collection is a part of an archive of photographs, journals, ephemera, etc. It contains six e-books on Glasgow and an additional five about Scotland. The Glasgow titles (original publication date in parenthesis) are: *Who's Who in Glasgow in 1909* (1909),

Glimpses of old Glasgow (1894), *Memoirs and portraits of one hundred Glasgow men* (1886), *Curiosities of Glasgow citizenship* (1881), *The old country houses of the old Glasgow gentry* (1878), and *The origin and history of Glasgow streets* (1902). The titles relating to Scotland are: *Scotland and the Antarctic* (2003), *Walking the Watershed* (1994), *Scotland in the nineteenth century* (1993), *Things seen in the Scottish Highlands* (1932), and *With nature and a camera* (1898) (which includes a chapter on 'How cage birds are caught: a day on Brighton Downs').

In each case the book is presented as a series of HTML pages – with images (maps, photographs, etc where appropriate) accessible from the contents pages; original pagination is indicated offset from the text. Some books have a facsimile of their covers.

48.   Global Text Project
Textbooks
http://globaltext.terry.uga.edu/books

A joint project of the Terry College of Business of the University of Georgia and The Daniels College of Business of the University of Denver, the Global Text Project plans to create a free library of 1,000 e-textbooks for students in developing world covering the range of topics typically encountered in a university's undergraduate programs. Their vision states that "Mass education has created tremendous opportunities and wealth for people in developed countries. It has enabled many to escape poverty, albeit a level of poverty that is not comparable to that of many in the developing nations. Mass education for the developing world is dependent among other things on finding low costs means of delivering free quality content to many. We believe we have the means for developing the necessary content and seek support to start an endeavor that can engage many for the benefit of many more. We will work through universities, world development agencies (e.g., World Bank, United Nations), and other appropriate bodies to promote adoption of the texts... Furthermore, we will work on creating a community that contributes to enhancement of the texts." All books are made available under a Creative Commons licence.

Books may be located from title listings under six subjects: Business; Computing; Education; Health; Science; and Social Science or brought together by searching on one or more of the narrower subject terms. Titles are listed with author(s) and a minimal description; they are also identified as a "Global Text book", a "Scanned book" or a "Link to another site". Those texts which are available on the Global Text site are almost all in PDF.

49.   Godfreys Book-shelf
Facsimiles
http://www.shipbrook.com/jeff/bookshelf/about.html

The Bookshelf contains facsimiles of books from the 15th to 19th centuries. Begun as an attempt by the owner to reclaim some space, in early 2010 the Bookshelf contained over 40 titles as PDF page images. The list may be sorted by title, author, subject, date, most recently added, and most popular. Selecting a title produces a neat table of bibliographic information, including a brief summary of the content, and clicking on the title-link downloads the PDF file. As may be expected with books of this age, some scanned pages are blemished or contain text which appears blurred. The collection includes ten music scores and five books of music instruction, including *Varietie of Lute-Lessons*, by Robert Dowland.

50.   Google Books
See also: **Google eBooks** (229)
Various
http://books.google.com/

There are two projects within Google Books, the Partner Program and the Library Project. The Partner Program works with publishers to make their titles discoverable.

The Library Project's aim is described as simply: to "make it easier for people to find relevant books – specifically, books they wouldn't find any other way such as those that are out of print and it is working with several major libraries to include their collections and show users information about the book, and in many cases... the search term in context." Library titles – both public domain and in-copyright books – are scanned. Copyright is respected by ensuring that when users find a book under copyright, they see only a card catalog-style entry providing basic information about the book and no more than two or three sentences of text surrounding the search term to help them determine whether they've found what they're looking for. Where books are out-of-copyright, or if the publisher or author has asked to make the book fully viewable, a Full View allows users to view any page from the book, and if the book is in the public domain, download, save and print a PDF version.

Gutenberg *see* **Project Gutenberg** *and* **Columbia University Press: gutenberg<e>**

51. Hans Christian Andersen
Fiction
http://hca.gilead.org.il/

The original translations into English of Hans Christian Andersen's 168 fairy tales was by H P Paull in 1872, and 140 of them are available in this collection. According to the introduction, this hypertext version is based both on an e-text found in the Andersen Homepage of the Danish National Literary Archive and on Mrs. Paull's nineteenth century translation, which is now in the public domain. The Danish National Literary Archive text is 'Danish Popular Legends' – "first published in *The Riverside Magazine for Young People*, Vol. IV, pp. 470-474, New York, October 1870, [and] never published in Denmark". All 168 tales are list chronologically on the home page.

Clicking on a title takes you to an individual page for the fable, in plain text across the complete screen width with black print against a grey background lightly illustrated by a repeat reproduction of a paper cutting made by Andersen of a Pierrot carrying a tray of object representing his own life. It is possible to switch off the background. At the foot of each tale are three arrows: back to the chronological list of titles, or to the previous and next titles. The initial letter of each tale is embellished by a small illustration.

52. HathiTrust
Various
http://www.hathitrust.org/

This shared digital repository for the thirteen universities of the Committee on Institutional Cooperation and the University of California system establishes a means for these universities to archive and share their digitised collections. At the time of review it contained some 6,622,028 volumes of which 3,838,821 are books. It should be noted that there seems to be no way of limiting searches to books.

The HathiTrust web site provides a portal with access tools for the content in the repository, and works with participating libraries to define, prioritise, and develop other tools and services. In April 2009 a temporary beta catalog was released, offering bibliographic searching (title, author, subject, ISBN, publisher, and year of publication) as well as faceted browsing of all items in the Library. Full-text searching searches across the content of all items, while browsing the collections offers access to subsets (such as the 47 adventure novels by G A Henty or the 2,760 titles in 'Ancestry and Genealogy') – many of which have been created as collections by users. Each collection can be listed in author, title or date order, each with links to the catalogue record or the full text of each. Some collections include items for which the 'full view' is not available (some items are limited, due to copyright restrictions, to 'search only'), in which case it is possible to limit the results to only the works available in full.

Individual facsimile pages of each work are presented with navigation for moving to previous/next, first/last and a numbered page, as well as via a Contents List to any chapter or section of the book. For each page it is possible to cycle through plain text, single-page PDF and the facsimile.

53.   Henrietta's Herbal
         Reference
         http://www.henriettesherbal.com/eclectic/index.html

The home page offers just over 40 classic herbal texts dating from the 1800s and early 1900s, one or two of which have yet to be added; other pages include: Eclectic; Physiomedicalist; Homeopathic; Allopathic; Deutsch; Svenska; and Suomeksi. By logging in to the site it is possible to run searches. Although works date from between 1817 (Bigelow, 1817-20: *American Medical Botany*) and 1936 (Harding, 1936: *Ginseng and Other Medicinal Plants*), it is stated that the works have been scanned and that they are "copyright © 2000-2010 Henriette Kress unless otherwise specified."

Works are first presented as a chapter list; individual chapters are presented as scrollable HTML pages. In some cases original illustrations are set within the page. The main menu remains visible in a left-hand column, and there are links to previous and next chapters, as well as 'Up' to the table of contents at the foot of each chapter page.

54.   Historical Mathematics Collection
Monographs
http://quod.lib.umich.edu/u/umhistmath/

The University of Michigan Historical Mathematics Collection contains nearly 1,000 books (many in German) selected from the University of Michigan mathematics collection that have been digitised to improve access and to preserve the content of these books. All of the books in this collection are from the 19th or early 20th century. The collection may be browsed (by title or author) or searched: using bibliographic details or Boolean logic and proximity searching of the full texts.

Selecting a title produces a formatted table with the author, title, publication information, availability and copyright, print source, and subject terms. Scrolling past these full bibliographic details, users come to buttons for purchase via Amazon, a long numerical list of individual page numbers, or a link for viewing the entire text. Selecting an individual page opens a PDF chapter at that page (there is no indication from the list where pages fall within chapters), while the entire text brings forth a long (sometimes very long – there is a warning about both the possible length and the quality of the OCR) HTML page.

55.   Ideology.us
Sociology, philosophy, psychology, education, politics
http://www.ideology.us/

Ideology.us offers direct access to fourteen titles. These are: René Descartes: *Discourse on Method*; Sigmund Freud: *Dream Psychology;* David Hume: *Human Understanding;* William James: *Pragmatism;* Ellen Key: *The Education of the Child;* Karl Marx and Friedrich Engels: *The Communist Manifesto;* John Stuart Mill: *On Liberty;* Friedrich Nietzsche: *Beyond Good and Evil;* George Bernard Shaw: *Parents and Children;* Mary Scharlieb and F. Arthur Sibly: *Youth and Sex;* Arthur Schopenhauer: *Studies in Pessimism;* Henry David Thoreau: *Civil Disobedience;* Elizabeth Towne: *Happiness and Marriage;* and Mary Wollstonecraft: *A Vindication of the Rights of Women*

As with Fiction.us (*see*), the link from the title leads to a contents page of chapters and individual chapters are clearly presented in dark blue text on an uncluttered white background. Unlike

Fiction.us, each chapter ends with links to the previous and next chapters, as well as to the table of contents.

56.   Internet Archive
        See also: **BookServer** and **Open Library**
        Various
        http://www.archive.org/details/texts

The Internet Archive (*see also* BookServer and Open Library) contains a wide range of fiction, popular books, children's books, historical texts and academic books. There are some 2,283,600 items, including over 1,269,000 in the American Libraries collection, 255,000 in the Canadian Libraries collection, 70,000 in the Universal Library Project (*see*, sometimes called the Million Books Project), 55,000 in the Open Source Books Project in which books are contributed by the community in a range of languages, 20,000 from Project Gutenberg (*see*), 3,300 in the Children's Library, and 41,600 from the Biodiversity Heritage Library (*see*). Many of the texts are of considerable antiquity, perhaps one of the older being *Homiliary on Gospels from Easter to first Sunday of Advent* by Heiric of Auxerre, ca. 841-ca. 876 – a manuscript in Latin on vellum.

Apart from selecting one of the sub-collections or one of the recently-reviewed or recently-added items from the home page, access is by a simple search (restricted to 'Texts' or one of the sub-collections) at the top of the home page or by an advanced search feature, which allows combinations of up to 11 terms, dates, collections, etc. When a title is selected from the search results, a page is returned containing a bibliographic record (including copyright status) with additional selected metadata and reviews (if any have been added), as well as the formats in which it may be downloaded. Normally these include: Read Online, PDF, ePub, Kindle, Daisy, full text, and DjVu. As with BookServer, PDF versions owned by the Internet Archive are scrollable files of facsimile pages, which may be printed or have images and/or text copied-and-pasted, however, for some books – notably those scanned by Google – the user will be passed to a separate server/web site and there may be different conditions.

57. Internet Sacred Text Archive
Various humanities/Religion
http://www.sacred-texts.com/

The Archive claims to be "the largest freely available archive of online books about religion, mythology, folklore and the esoteric on the Internet... dedicated to religious tolerance and scholarship." The topics listed on the home page range from Age of Reason to Zoroastrianism by way of Astrology, Christianity, Earth Mysteries, Hinduism, Tarot, and Tolkein (the texts and sagas used as inspiration for his work). The home page also offers a Google search facility, some popular searches, a few newly-added titles, and a link to 'Catalog' from which you can search titles, author or subjects, or browse full titles, full author names or title, author or subject keywords. Browsing any of the lists makes it immediately clear how wide ranging is the content in this archive.

Some texts open at a contents page while others take readers directly to the text. Both pages, like the alphabetic lists of titles, etc which can be browsed, are simple, scrollable HTML pages with minimal formatting. In the texts, the original pagination is indicated.

DVDs of Sacred texts are also available from the site.

58. Jane Austen's Fiction Manuscripts
Manuscripts
http://www.janeausten.ac.uk/index.html

The manuscripts have been digitised to the highest possible standard with images for *Volume the First* provided by the Bodleian Library, and for *Volume the Second*, *Volume the Third*, *Persuasion*, and *Opinions of Mansfield Park and Emma* by the British Library, the project partners, while other manuscripts have been provided by their owners. The 'Introduction to the Edition' notes that the manuscripts are "[l]aid out in conscious imitation or parody of the formal features of book design, and labelled by Austen *Volume the First*, *Volume the Second*, and *Volume the Third*." No manuscripts have been located for works which saw publication in Jane Austen's lifetime (*Sense and Sensibility*, *Pride and Prejudice*, *Mansfield Park*, *Emma*, *Northanger Abbey* or *Persuasion*) and it supposed that she destroyed them as each book was published. There is a considerable amount of documentation on the site detailing methodologies, editorial principles, technical notes and conservation issues; and each manuscript has a 'Head Note' essay offering a general description, "an account of the provenance and history of its ownership; a physical description of the manuscript as a document or object and a technical analysis or collation of its structures; [and] a description of the manuscript's contents."

Each manuscript can be displayed as a series of thumbnail facsimiles, as 'Diplomatic Display' in which there are parallel (to the left and right of the screen) text and full-size facsimile or as facsimile-only – in which case each page is shown with a rule, a colour scale, and can be magnified, moved around the screen area and examined in some detail. Access is by individual manuscript, although an intelligent search function offers access across the collection.

59.   Libertary: Freedom of the Book
Various
http://www.libertary.com/

Like BookGlutton (*see*) the Libertary collection provides a platform for social reading; unlike BookGlutton this is not currently done alongside the page being read but in separate discussion fora for each book. The home page offers a few featured titles and access to the collection through eight categories: Politics - History - Business - Law; Health - Science - Technology; Fiction - Poetry - Memoir; Self Help - Inspirational; Instructional - How To; Entertainment - Sports; Religion - Philosophy and Other; or by way of an author list, a title list, new titles, or searching for authors or titles.

From the brief listings (a Google-like title, author and abbreviated first sentence of an abstract), there is a link to a summary page with the full description, a cover image and the chance to purchase the book. In the left-hand column is a chapter list leading to the full text of each chapter, a search facility for the full text of the book, and a link to the book's discussion forum.

Chapters are presented as single scrollable HTML pages with the print-copy pagination shown. The left-hand column remains so that access to other chapters is immediate, as is searching or links to the discussions.

60.   Library of Congress Country Studies
        See also: **CIA World Fact Book**
        Handbooks
        http://lcweb2.loc.gov/frd/cs/cshome.html

The site is described on its home page as containing "the online versions of books previously published (1988-98) in hard copy by the Federal Research Division of the Library of Congress under the Country Studies/Area Handbook Program sponsored by the U.S. Department of the Army. Because the original intent of the series' sponsor was to focus primarily on lesser-known areas of the world or regions in which U.S. forces might be deployed, the series is not all-inclusive. At present, 101 countries and regions are covered. The date of information for each country appears on the title page of each country and at the end of each section of text." The Country Studies present descriptions and analyses of the historical setting and the social, economic, political, and national security systems and institutions of these countries. Although in early 2010, country studies of Iran and North Korea had just been published, these countries are only covered electronically by late 1980's/early 1990's editions. The site contains only earlier editions, and due to funding difficulties no new handbooks are planned.

Visitors to each volume are first presented with a lengthy Contents page from which in the region of 250 chapter sections and sub-sections can be accessed. Each of these sections has quick navigation to next and previous sections, as well as to the Table of Contents. Some countries have no tabular information because it was not available in electronic format and has not been added to the text.

The text is not copyrighted.

**61.   Library of Western Fur Trade Historical Source
        Documents**
        Historical
        http://www.xmission.com/~drudy/mtman/mmarch.html

This archive contains over forty texts which are accounts of the Rocky Mountain fur trade during the first half of the 19th century; there are both primary and secondary sources; that is, those written by, or told by those who were actually there. Not all are books; there are, for example, accounts of travels published by newspapers; in other cases a title such as Peter Skene Ogden's

Snake Country Journals may lead to several volumes. Some of the books have been donated by the Project Gutenberg (*see*).

Multi-volume titles lead to a brief introduction – possibly with an illustration – and links to the discrete volumes; where there is only a single volume the link leads directly to a single HTML page containing the entire text.

62.   Literature Network
Literature
http://www.online-literature.com/

The Literature Network offers access to a huge catalogue of English literature on a site that is heavily supported by advertisements – including a pop-up browser window when first entering the site. Apart from direct links to the Bible and Shakespeare, access is via an alphabetic author list – a single, 3-column page of about 260 authors. There is no explanation of the provenance of the works included other than the statement, "We offer searchable online literature for the student, educator, or enthusiast." The works appear to be out-of-copyright editions (although this may not be true of the site's editorial content).

Author pages contain a picture of the author, and give a short biography/summary of writings, dotted with pictorial advertisements, with a list of works to the left. It is possible to search all of the author's works, and at the foot of some author pages are 'Related Links'; 'Articles on [author]'; and 'Quizzes on [author]' – many of these links are to remote web pages. There are also recent Forum posts on the author – these are mainly essay- and homework-help queries.

The link to an author's work offers a similar page from which the individual work can be searched and links and forum posts relating to the individual title can be viewed. In the left-hand column are listed the chapters of, or poems in, the book. Each chapter is a long scrollable HTML page, and again the text is interspersed with pictorial advertisements. At the top and foot of the page it is possible to navigate backwards – that is to that work's main page, the list of authors or the Literature Network's home page – and there is no direct navigation link to the next chapter; however the vertical word 'MENU' against the left page margin slides down the page and remains visible as the page is scrolled, and offers direct access to all other chapter.

It is possible to subscribe to the site for advert-free reading experience.

63.   Literature Project
     Literature
     http://www.literatureproject.com/

The Literature Project provides immediate access to a limited collection of 'classic' books, poems, speeches and plays. For each item, a table of contents/chapter list offers access to the free online e-book. In addition, each book's top page includes a link to a list of cheap (typically less than US$10) downloadable versions of the e-book in a range of formats from eBookMall. In all there are around eighty of the out-of-copyright titles most often found on the Web listed on the home page: *The Adventures of Tom Sawyer, Black Beauty, Dracula, The Iliad, Persuasion, The Time Machine* and so on, although a few less usual titles such as *The Sketch Book of Geoffrey Crayon, Gent.* by Washington Irving and *Main Street* by Sinclair Lewis were also listed. Material on the site is copyright to the Literature Project and the terms of use allow only personal use.

Beneath the title list on the home page, and similarly placed in the table of contents and chapter pages, are links to 'Recommended eBooks', 'Directories', 'Search' and 'Terms of Use'. Beneath this at the foot of the home and all successive pages is a list of some "Great Sites" for further access to e-books. Recommendations can be browsed by format (for example Adobe PDF, Microsoft Reader, Palm), category (Art & Music; Cooking, Food & Wine; etc), title or author; however these e-books are for purchase from eBookMall, many at a greater price than suggested above for the home-page titles. 'Directories' offers a short list of e-book sites, and Search, which claims to offer Boolean searching within the texts, does not appear to work.

Book chapters are presented full screen width, black type on a plain white background with links to 'Prev[ious]', 'Next' and 'Contents' at the head and beneath the text (before the links).

Llyfrau O'r Gorffennol *see* **Books from the Past**

64.   Logos Library
Various multilingual
http://www.logoslibrary.eu/

The Logos Library (there is a separate Children's Logos Library. *See*) functions as a powerful interface to novels, technical literature and translated texts in many languages, offering access by way of a massive database of over 707,737,941 words. Searching on any word produces a word-in-context display of matching texts, which can then be read online – either within Logos or at their original location. It is also possible to select a language from the home page to move to an author/title listing. There are 44,778 titles in some 111 languages including Afrikaans, Faeroese, Mongolian and Welsh (over 4,600 in English).
Selecting a book produces a slightly curious display in which the central column (less than 50% of the total screen width) is given over to the text and some up and down arrows which move to next or previous pages. As the column is so narrow, there are often irregular line breaks followed by one-word or very short lines. Books may also be downloaded.

The home page also offers links to the Children's Logos Library, a children's dictionary, crossword and anagram help and other tools.

65.   Making of America
Historic texts
http://quod.lib.umich.edu/m/moa/

This University of Michigan site – the result of an Andrew W. Mellon Foundation project – describes itself as, "a digital library of primary sources in American social history primarily from the antebellum period through reconstruction. The collection is particularly strong in the subject areas of education, psychology, American history, sociology, religion, and science and technology. The book collection currently contains approximately 10,000 books with 19th century imprints." A partner in the project, Cornell University, concentrated on serials for the same period.

Books can be browsed by title, author or subject (subject are hierarchical, so that although 'African Americans' shows six hits, selecting it shows a list of 22 titles including 'African Americans – Education' etc. The title list (which can be sorted by 5 criteria) gives a brief bibliographic record with subject keywords for each title, plus buttons to 'Order a hardcover' and 'Order a softcover at Amazon.com' and links to 'List all pages', 'View first page' and 'Add to bookbag' – an online record of search finds, which can be emailed or downloaded for future use. 'List all pages' gives a full bibliographic record, including print source and availability, as well as a list giving access to individual pages. Clicking on the first (or any) page produces a facsimile of the page with previous and next buttons, as well as the ability to change the image size, move directly to another page or search the text. In addition to the image, a page can be viewed as text or PDF. A print button presents a clean page image (no navigation, etc) in another browser tab or window ready for printing.

66.   **ManyBooks**
       Fiction
       http://manybooks.net/

ManyBooks – "the best books at the best price: free!" is run by Matthew McClintock and offers (in early 2010) more than 26,000 free e-books, which may be listed by author, title, language (36, from Afrikaans to Welsh, including Esperanto, Latin, Maori and Middle English) or category (62, including Government Publications, Harvard Classics, and Instructional as well as genres such as Mystery, Romance and Espionage, and types such as Fiction, Non-fiction, and Reference) – the home page also offers new titles, recommended titles, books of the week, and a 'spotlight' title. There is also a RSS feed to keep you up-to-date. The 'About the Site' page notes that, "Many of the etexts are from the November, 2003 Project Gutenberg DVD, which contains the entire Project Gutenberg (see) archives except for the Human Genome Project and audio eBooks, due to size limitations, and the Project Gutenberg of Australia (see) eBooks, due to copyright. As of July 2004 most current Gutenberg texts are available here, usually within the week of release. There are also public domain and creative commons works from many other sources."

When a title is chosen, users are given a brief summary plus information on language, author, publication date, word and page counts, series, genres and the number of times the book has been downloaded. When relevant there are links to other titles by the author, in the series, in the language, etc. From the summary page, books can be downloaded in a wide range of formats.

67. MERLOT: Multimedia Educational Resource for Learning and Online Teaching
Textbooks
http://www.merlot.org/merlot/index.htm

As its name implies, there is much more than e-books in MERLOT, but nearly all subject collections of teaching resources includes access to a number of 'Open Textbooks'. Many of these take the form of a Wiki, others are a simple HTML web page, but all seem to be located on remote sites (e.g. Connexions (*see*) or Wikibooks (*see*)), MERLOT acting as a gateway. Textbooks vary in size quite considerably – some are divided into chapters and sub-sections, while other are briefer and more like lecture notes.

Each summary record includes the date that the resource was added to MERLOT, a date modified, author, a single sentence of context (which may be the first sentence of the text), and a peer-review with a star rating (or "Not reviewed"). Some resources also have a 'MERLOT Editor's Choice' or a 'MERLOT Classics' badge.

Visiting one of the seven subject collections (Art, Business, Education, etc) takes users directly to a long list of mixed resources, which can be refined by selecting a material type (e.g. animation, case study, open textbook, tutorial) from the left-hand column. They can also be broken down into sub-genres, for example art textbooks include: Art History (4), Cinema (1), Fine Arts (3), Music (4), Photography (1), and Theatre (1). Also from the home page, it is possible to move to a Discipline Community (Biology, Business, Chemistry, Criminal Justice, etc); from these pages it is ten necessary to move on to their 'Learning Materials Area', where again the resources can be limited to textbooks.

Million Books Project *see* **Digital Library of India**

68. Missouri Botanic Gardens Rare Books
Antiquarian botanic
http://www.illustratedgarden.org/mobot/rarebooks/

A part of the Biodiversity Heritage Library (*see*), the Missouri Botanic Gardens also offers access to its rare books in its own right. Over 60 titles or in excess of 100 authors can be browsed or searched by common or scientific plant names. As most books are illustrated, it is also possible to purchase collections of prints.

Selecting a book produces a page offering direct access to the Introduction, possible a list of volumes, bibliographic information, a link to view the pages, 'Structure' (basically, a list of pages offering direct access to each), a list of illustrations and a view using the Botanicus (see) interface. It is possible to sort the list of illustrations by common or either name as printed or current scientific names, and many illustrations have additional 'Plant information'. View pages offers thumbnail illustrations of eight pages at a time from which to select a starting point. The full facsimile page offers previous and next buttons as well as a 'View in Detail' button offering the Botanicus facility to rotate, magnify and move around the page. If the page contains an illustration, there may also be a link to further plant information.

69.   MobileRead
Various
http://www.mobileread.com/

In addition to various online forums which discuss e-book publishing, the site offers (from 'E-Books' on the top menu bar) access to public domain and often out-of-copyright e-books, predominantly in Mobipocket, Sony BBeB, ePub and eBookwise formats. Each title is listed with an indication of its genre (e.g. Historical fiction, Other fiction, Young adult, Children) and when selected is introduced by an author biography and/or a quotation from the introduction or a synopsis of the plot. Additionally, a cover image is usually provided. Some books are noted as being public domain in a particular country and users are warned "If the book is under copyright in your country, do not download or redistribute this work". Books must be downloaded to the relevant handheld e-book reader. There are an estimated 5,000 titles available. The site also provides a regularly updated *Mobipocket Download Guide.*

70.   Mobipocket Free e-Books
Various
http://www.mobipocket.com/freebooks/default.aspx

Until recently, the site offered well over 11,000 free e-books in a variety of languages. In 2010, Mobipocket first confronted the prospective user with five pages of 'New Arrivals': the 100 latest titles to be added. To the left were language and subject subdivisions (mostly literature and history), as well as a search box, which could be limited to the English language. There seemed to be no easy way of displaying all of the subjects covered as the narrow column of the display listed only about 20 subject divisions at a time; in any event some caution seems indicated in relying totally on the classifications. The three entries, 'Diaries'; 'Pepys, Samuel 1633-1703' and 'Pepys, Samuel 1633-1703 Diaries' all lay claim to 82 titles, but a search for 'Diary' (in English language) located 101 titles. All free books were out-of-copyright editions. Another area of the site makes available e-books for purchase.

As may be divined from the site's name, only one format is offered – mobi – but this software works on a number of dedicated readers such as Amazon's Kindle (since 2005, Mobipocket has been an Amazon company), the Cybook and the iRex as well as on many smartphones; and the PC software can be downloaded from the site for free.

Listings of titles presented minimal information for each – title, author (with dates), Language (indicated by a flag), the date that this version of the e-book file was created, and file size – and clicking on the title image has the same effect as the 'Download book' button.

Early in 2011, the above URL and the link to 'Download free eBooks' on the home page (http://www.mobipocket.com/) both lead to a completely empty page headed 'Free eBooks by MOBIPOCKET Amazon.com'. It seems as though the site is undergoing maintenance, although the home page still offers e-books for sale and a linked page offers discounts of between 20% and 80% on a range of titles.

71. Munsey's Blackmask
Various
http://www.munseys.com/site/home

Munsey's provide the front pages to the site which enable a book to be selected, read about (some books have reader reviews in addition to the synopsis) and downloaded; access for online reading (HTML) is provided by their Blackmask Online pages, now available at the munceys.com URL. Some 20,000 books are categorised variously as: Action; Australia; Biography; Canada; Children; Classic; Comics; Critics; Drama; Education; Elizabethans; Enlightenment; Esoteric; Europa; Fiction; Folklore; History; Horror; Illustrated; Liberal Arts; Mystery; Nautical; Nonfiction; Orient Express; Periodicals; Philosophy; Poetry;

Political; Science; Pulp Fiction; Reference; Religion; Renaissance; Satire; Science; Science Fiction; and Travel. Munsey's offers the following formats: Daisy, eBookwise, Plucker, Rocket eBook, Isilo, Adobe Acrobat (PDF), Sony Reader, Mobipocket/Kindle, MS-Reader, Zipped, and Adobe ePub.

72. New York Botanical Garden, The LuEsther T. Mertz Library Rare Book Digitization Project
Various
http://mertzdigital.nybg.org/

The LuEsther T. Mertz Library is an important botanical and horticultural research library, and has digitised and made freely available some parts of its collections; the Library is a major contributor to the Biodiversity Heritage Library (*see*). The e-book collections available are: Latin American Plant Literature; the Nathaniel and Elizabeth Button Archives; Rare Books and Manuscripts; Collectors' Field Notebooks; Books on Trees; Landscape Architecture and Urban Parks; Plant Lists; Seed Catalogs; and Other Books. Titles in each collection may be browsed, in which case cover images, titles, publication dates, subject terms and descriptions are listed, or all or any of the collections can be searched using Boolean logic, word adjacency or field searching.

Books are opened in what is becoming the quasi-standard screen layout for e-books with a page list and search in the left-hand column and the facsimile pages to the right. Pages may be zoomed, fitted to the screen area, or rotated; and it is also possible to view a thumbnail image in the left-hand column and to 'clip' the main image into another browser window where it can be cropped, e-mailed or printed. Both the document and the individual page being viewed can be added to favourites/bookmarks and a separate button pops up the 'reference URL' for the page.

73. Open Access Textbooks Project
Textbooks
http://www.openaccesstextbooks.org/

The US Fund for the Improvement of Postsecondary Education (FIPSE) has funded this two-year initiative. The Open Access Textbooks Project is working with others organisations to develop a sustainable model to discover, produce, and disseminate open access textbooks.

At present, the project site is limited to providing around two dozen links to a number of other sites which provide access to textbooks, such as Bookboon (*see*), Connexions (see), FreeBooks4Doctors (*see*), FreeTechBooks (*see*), Wikibooks (*see*), etc.

74.   Open Book Project
Textbooks
http://openbookproject.net/

The Open Book Project home page states that it "is aimed at the educational community and seeks to encourage and coordinate collaboration among students and teachers for the development of high quality, freely distributable textbooks and educational materials on a wide range of topics." This statement means effectively that educational materials made available on the site are 'Copyleft' or in the public domain, thus ensuring that they remain freely available, and that the software used in the textbooks is covered by the GNU General Public License (or similar). The site owners claim to support the equality of languages by making material available in as many languages as possible.

Although there is nothing in the mission statement to indicate a subject orientation, the site is currently devoted to electronics and computer science. At the time of writing there are only three titles or series available: *How to Think Like a Computer Scientist* (Allen B. Downey *et al.*) – an introductory computer science text book available in several programming and natural languages; *How to Think Like a Computer Scientist: Learning with Python* (Jeffrey Elkner *et al.*) – an introductory computer science text book using Python; and *Lessons in Electric Circuits* (Tony R. Kuphaldt) – a series of textbooks on the subjects of electricity and electronics.

In addition to e-books, there are Tutorials, Courses and Projects.

75. Open Library
Literature
http://www.openlibrary.org/ and (March 2010, a newly designed version of the site, offered for public testing): http://upstream.openlibrary.org/

This, like the BookServer (*see*), is a project of the Internet Archive (*see*). Although this is still described as a Beta Site and there is a message on the home page which talks about maintaining the site at a "special URL until we're sure it's stable enough to make the final transition to openlibrary.org", not only is access at that URL but the site contains almost 24,000,000 titles of which over 1,167,000 are available in full text. The basic records have been gathered from catalogues and from individual input. The intention is to have one web page for every book ever published – a target which the owners see as possible. These records link to full-text scanned facsimiles of the original books stored in the Internet Archive – often originating from the Google Books Project. The Open Library is a project of the Internet Archive, funded in part by grants from the California State Library and the Kahle/Austin Foundation.

The home page offers a simple search, which can be limited to the scanned books and an Advanced Search which allows searching by title, author, subject, publisher and ISBN in addition to limiting by a date range and to scanned books. There is no browse facility. Entering an unrestricted simple search such as "letters" produces a results page listing which defaults to titles with small cover images and minimal information (title, author, date of publication); the alternative is larger cover images with no further information. In either case there is the option – in the left-hand column – to limit the results in a variety of ways. All of the limits have an existing results figure following them so that it is clear what will happen should the search be limited by any of the following: availability or non-availability of full text; individual authors and subjects; publication date range, language or publishers. Selecting a full-text title produces a bibliographic record including as much information as is available, possibly including the book size and weight, ISBNs, cataloguing data, availability via e.g. Amazon or local libraries (WorldCat data) and a 'Read Online' button. Because this is 'open' project there are also buttons enabling users to change the cover image, and add or edit the description or the Table of Contents.

Reading each e-book is by way of the facsimile images stored in the Internet Archive, which can be zoomed and read in single- or double-page view. There are buttons to move to the first, last, next and previous pages, and – if in the double-page view – clicking on the edge of a page will turn the pages virtually. Beside the pages is a simple 'search in book' facility. The only problem with the parallel worlds of the Open Library and the Internet Archive is that – at the time of writing – there is no way back to the Open Library from the facsimile book; the only link is to the Internet Archive.

The Open Library site also offers users the opportunity to add book records.

76. Orange Grove Open Textbooks
Textbooks
http://florida.theorangegrove.org/og/access/home.do

Florida's Digital Repository contains a number of collections, including the Orange Grove Resources, including 197 open textbooks. This collection can be searched using phrases, wild cards and Boolean logic to produce subject results listing titles with brief descriptions, format and a link to full details. The full details page includes a full description, author, creator, subject keywords, language, format, interactivity type, learning resource type, educational context or level and ERIC Thesaurus keywords, as well as a copyright statement. In some cases the content link (either from the title in the original list or from the details page) leads to a licence agreement with 'Reject' and 'Preview' buttons.

Most – but not all – texts are PDF files.

77. Oriental Institute of the University of Chicago
Scholarly texts
https://oi.uchicago.edu/research/pubs/catalog/

There are some fourteen series of titles (including for example, *The Demotic Dictionary of the Oriental Institute of the University of Chicago* and the Oriental Institute Digital Archives), and subject access to further titles in Anatolian Studies; Archaeology; Egypt; Epigraphic Survey; Hittite Civilization; Islamic Studies; Language and Text Studies; Mesopotamian Civilization; Nubian Civilization; Iranian Civilization; Prehistoric Near East; and Syro/Palestine. Titles date back 1997. Not all are freely available but icons in title / author / year of publication listings indicate the availability of a free PDF version and/or a copy for purchase. Where PDF versions are available, there is also a link to a standard 'Terms of Use' page.

78.   Oxford Text Archive
Various humanities
http://ota.ahds.ac.uk/

The Oxford Text Archive (OTA) collects, catalogues and preserves electronic literary and linguistic resources for use in education, in research, teaching and learning. Not all titles are freely available and some may not appear in the title listings as they were deposited for preservation purposes only. The archive holds many thousands of texts in over 25 different languages.

There is a simple search facility or a columnar, browsable list which can be sorted by availability, title, language and author. Works are *only* available for downloading, in some cases this may mean HTML but in others the work may be in plain text, OCP markup, COCOA markup, etc.

Clicking on an ID number of a free work produces a detailed bibliographic record, including title, author, availability, language, editorial practice (which will state the format), OTA keywords, Library of Congress keywords, extent (file size), creation date, a source description and notes. Clicking on the link to the work will produce a page of terms and conditions, which must be acknowledged by entering your e-mail address. The link to the file will be sent to that address.

79.   Page by Page Books
Literature
http://www.pagebypagebooks.com/

This simple site offers three listings of "all the books we have available" – two alphabetically arranged title or author/title lists, each divided into eight divisions, and a third listing of authors allowing access to author pages with lists of titles: "All these books you can read now, for free! Catch up on your reading list, expand your horizons, or just spend a relaxing evening by yourself". The home page also includes a Google site search. The title lists includes occasional brief descriptions of books. Selecting any title produces a simple contents page from which individual chapters or sections can be selected. Chapters are presented as a series of HTML (web) pages of text, with buttons for next page, contents, and previous and next chapters, as well as links to further books by the author and more books. The site recommends this approach as being a more manageable way to read, as it offers the ability to bookmark by page rather than by chapter or whole book.

There is nothing to explain the selection of titles on the site, but they are clearly all out-of-copyright or public domain works although Page By Page Books has copyright to the HTML versions and editorial changes to the books on our site. Authors include John Adams, Emile Bronte, George W Bush and William Jefferson Clinton (inaugural addresses), Stephen Crane, Charles Dickens, and so on past Huxley, London and Plato to P G Wodehouse – although often all of their works are not included.

The site is supported by Google Ads.

80.   Palimpsest onLine
Various
http://www2.hn.psu.edu/faculty/jmanis/jimspdf.htm

Palimpsest onLine is Penn State University's Electronic Classics Site. The available texts include original work published in hard copy by the Pennsylvania State University and classical works of literature in English. Eighty-five authors (or works – the Bible, Qu'ran, Codex Junius II, and one or two other works are also listed by title) are listed. Selecting any of these leads to a 'front page' listing the available works with their sizes in pages and Kbytes. In some cases titles are available in two page sizes. Annoyingly whenever you leave these pages there is a pop-up message reminding you to bookmark the page.

During the review of this site the PDF files consistently stopped loading so that any comments on the e-books themselves cannot be made.

81.   Perseus Digital Library (also known as **The Perseus Hopper**)
Classics
http://www.perseus.tufts.edu/

The Perseus Library is both a practical experiment to explore possibilities and challenges of digital collections in a networked world and the beginnings of a full record of humanity – linguistic sources, physical artifacts, historical spaces – preserved for "every human being, regardless of linguistic or cultural background." From the Collections page, it can be seen that the largest collections are the classical and the 19th-century American (each at around 60,000,000 words), Arabic materials boast about a million words, and there are 4,737,070 words from papyri. Oddly, although words are counted, titles are not.

It is possible to search across all collections or to browse titles in each collection separately. On entering a collection there is a table indicating languages, so that, for example, in the American collection there are 58,324,864 words in English compared to just 2,638 words in French. Each title is listed by author with two links – one to the title and one offering 'Search this work' which links to a comprehensive advanced search tool.

The page for viewing the e-book is divided into three columns: the left column (approximately one-fifth width) contains an expandable table of contents (e.g. Chapter 2, may be divided into page 13, page 14, etc), while the text appears in the next two-fifths of the screen. The right-hand column has lists of automatically extracted place names (in some cases it is possible to view a map of the most frequently mentioned places) and people, and references. Across the top of the page is a graphic illustration/browser bar showing progress: the chapter and page being viewed within the whole text. If an entire chapter is selected it must be scrolled through and then another chapter selected from the table of contents; similarly with pages (although in this case there is less scrolling but more returns to the table of contents).

82.   Planet eBook
    Classic literature
    http://www.planetebook.com/

Planet eBook makes classic literature available as free PDF downloads, which users are encouraged to share. In fact most books also contain a link within their PDF bookmarks/contents page back to the web site information on sharing: you may share the book in any way so long as no charge is made for it. All books are licensed under a Creative Commons Attribution-Noncommercial 3.0 United States License.

What makes a book 'classic literature' for Planet eBook is not explained, but the titles include those one might expect: *Wuthoring Heights, Anna Karenina, David Copperfield, Around* the World in 80 Days, Dracula, Erewhon, Sons and Lovers, The Idiot, and so on. Selecting any of the 60+ titles on the home page takes users to a page with title, author, publication date and the first page of the text, as well as buttons for downloading in a '1-page version' or a '2-page version': the latter seeming to be stored as double-page spreads, although this makes no difference to the display on the screen. All books include links via the PDF bookmarks to each chapter or section.

The site is supported by Google Ads. There is also a blog, an e-mail newsletter and the possibility of suggesting a new title.

83. PoemHunter.com: Free Poetry eBooks
Poetry
http://www.poemhunter.com/eBooks/

Part of a larger site offering access to poetry, the e-books pages offer access to fully navigable PDF e-books. The site contains 336 pages, or around 6,700, e-books by poets as diverse as Roald Dahl and Emily Dickinson; Rabindranath Tagore and Khalil Gibran; Haniel Long and Pablo Neruda. Unfortunately the site has no search facility so access is by browsing successive pages of the contents. The number of poems and the file size is given for each poetry e-book: some titles have only one or two poems, others contain more than 1,000. In all cases the books are derived from the PoemHunter database (also available on the web site).

Most – but not all – collections begin with a biographical note about the poet; all have a plain title page/cover showing, for example, "Classic Poetry Series / Walt Whitman / - Poems - / Publication Date: / 2004 / Publisher: / PoemHunter.Com – The World's Poetry Archive" and provide access to individual poems by way of the PDF bookmarks/contents page.

Editorial quality cannot be guaranteed, as can be seen in the first verse from one of Emily Dickinson's poems (entitled "'Heaven" — is what I cannot reach!' in the associated database) where the em-dash is used correctly throughout the poem, but is transcribed in the book as '—' for each occurrence:
    "Heaven"—is what I cannot reach!
    The Apple on the Tree—
    Provided it do hopeless—hang—
    That—"Heaven" is—to Me!

84.   Potto
Textbooks
http://www.potto.org/

The Potto Project is described as a collaborative effort to write quality textbooks for colleges, and operates in the spirit of the open-content movement. There are four textbooks:

- o   Dr. Genick Bar-Meir: *Fundamentals of Compressible Flow Mechanics.* December 2008. Available in several formats including complete and chapter PDFs and DVi and LaTeX, it is also possible to order the hard copy book.
- o   Dr. Genick Bar-Meir: *Fundamentals of Die Casting Design.* 2009. Available as PDF, DVI, LaTeX and PostScript.
- o   Dr. Genick Bar-Meir: *Basics of Fluid Mechanics.* January 2010. Available in several formats including complete and chapter PDFs and DVi and LaTeX.
- o   Dr. Genick Bar-Meir: *Additional Material* (Masters Thesis). May 2009. Available as PDF.

According to the introduction to the three main books, eight further textbooks will follow: *Dynamics, Heat Transfer, Mechanics, Open Channel Flow, Statics, Strength of Material, Thermodynamics,* and *Two/Multi phases flow.*

85.   Project Gutenberg
Various humanities
http://www.gutenberg.org/catalog/

The oldest archive of e-books, Project Gutenberg carries over 33,000 free e-books to read on your PC, iPad, Kindle, Sony Reader, iPhone, Android or other portable device, in addition to a further 100,000 titles available from project partners: sister projects such as Project Gutenberg of Australia or affiliates such as the Online Books Page (*see*). From the catalogue page, it is possible to perform author, title or e-text number searches, or to browse by author, title or language; languages are divided between those with fewer than 50 books and those with more – selecting English produces the message, "There are too many English books to list them in one page. Please use the Browse-By-Author pages instead."

As with the Oxford Text Archive (*see*), e-books must be downloaded in order to be read. Selecting a title offers details of the author, translator and title; subject terms, language, e-text number and release date; and copyright status. It is possible to link directly to other works by the author or translator. Beneath this are links for downloading the title in a range of formats including plain text and some of HTML, ePub, Unicode, Mobipocket, etc. In some cases a mirror site is offered as an alternative source. An HTML download produces a single long page, topped by a chapter or section list from which it is possible to move directly to fixed points in the page.

86. Project Gutenberg of ...
Australia
> http://gutenberg.net.au/

Canada
> http://www.gutenberg.ca/

Germany
> http://gutenberg.spiegel.de/
> Various humanities

These sites provide books which are in the public domain in each country and function broadly in the same way as the master site, although in some cases the e-book can be read online.

87. Project Runeberg
> *See also:* **Project Gutenberg**
> Scandinavian/Nordic literature
> http://runeberg.org/

A sister project of Project Gutenberg (*see*), Project Runeberg is based at LYSATOR, the students' computer club at Linköping University in Linköping, Sweden. The alphabetic title listing in the catalogue offers direct links to other works by the author, a note of the publication date and the language, and – by clicking on the title – access to the text; almost uniquely among free e-book collections, there are MARC records for some titles. Unlike Project Gutenberg, there is no facility for downloading but individual pages of the e-book are linked from a contents page. Individual pages are facsimiles followed by their OCR text. In some cases, apart from the default format there may be monochrome and colour PDF versions and a full-resolution JPEG file for a page. Navigation is to previous/next pages or back to the table of contents.

88.   Public Literature
Various
http://publicliterature.org/

Moving to any of the links around the list of around 300 classic titles listed on the home page, takes readers to a series of blogs: Article, Book Review, Children's, Classics, Comedy, Fiction, News, Non-Fiction, Play, Poetry, Sci-Fi, Uncategorized and Writing. Some posts are poems and some are written by authors such as Paulo Coelho.

The table of e-books offers the chance to read on the screen or – unusually – to listen, as around 90% of them may be read aloud. Most of the usual 'classic' authors are to be found, but in addition there are Vonnegut, Freud and Nietzsche, as well as the Bible and titles including *Short History of Wales* (and France, Holland, the United States, etc), *Manual of Egyptian Archeaology and Guide to the Study of Antiquities in Egypt, Democracy in America* (de Tocqueville), *Magna Carta,* and *Selected Letters of Beethoven.*

Clicking on either the title or the 'Read Online' symbol produces a page-by-page presentation, with – to the right – a note of books recently started, related available titles and the facility to download the current e-book as some or all of: a text file, in PDF, or as an audio or Kindle book; a 'Hardcopy' button takes you to Amazon. There is also a literature timeline and the Google translation tool. The page text is presented in Courier font and, being equivalent to approximately two print pages, requires some scrolling to complete. At the foot of the page is a 'Next Page' button. From the top of the page of text it is possible to click on the loudspeaker symbol to hear the LibriVox recording (free audio books read by volunteers with the goal of recording every book in the public domain), or on 'Get the Book' link which also takes you to Amazon. The LibriVox recording available from the home page or from within the book opens a thin orange bar across the top of the page which enables the reading to be paused, resumed, and moved ahead or back, as well as the volume to be controlled.

### 89.	ReadPrint
Literature
http://www.readprint.com/

ReadPrint offers a library of over 8,000 free e-books by 3,500 authors "absolutely free for students, teachers, and the classic enthusiast". It notes that is has been seen on BBC World, CNN and USA Today! The home page lists top authors and top books as well as offering browsing by author and a search box.

Selecting an author from the browse index produces either, where there are no digitised e-books available, one or more quotations by the author, or a list of books plus quotations and in some cases a short biographical note, a full biography and an image of the author. Searching is via a Google custom search and produces some annoying Ads. By Google above and also to the right of occurrences of the search term in titles, chapter titles, author names, etc

Selecting a title produces a contents page from which a chapter (or a poem) may be selected. There are two modes for reading – the default HTML page has a centre column of black on white text with links on the left leading back to the title (chapter list) and back to the author page. The entire chapter can then be scrolled through and ends with a button to lead to the following chapter. There is also a button to 'Launch Reading Mode' at the top of each chapter. Reading Mode produces a black background devoid of all distractions, with an inner scrollable window containing the chapter in black text on a beige background, but although this is clearly intended for easy reading, here there is no end button leading to the following chapter.

### 90.	Read Classic Books Online (Classic Reader)
Literature
http://www.classicreader.com/

The Classic Reader web site is published by Blackdog Media, a one-person company run by Stephane Theroux, in British Columbia, and went live early in 2000. All books published on the Classic Reader web site are in the public domain (out of copyright) and thus may be used freely. All of the books in the Classic Reader collection are the full unabridged versions. The site admits that there is no set system for the selection of books added to the collection and that they are chosen more or less at random. Some of the titles in the collection are added at the suggestion of visitors to the site.

From the home page you can move to one of eight categories (Fiction, Non-Fiction, Shakespeare, Short Stories, Young Readers, Drama, Poetry, and Classical), browse by author or title; or use the simple search box which searches the full text of the library. A few recent titles and authors are also listed. In March 2010, the site included 3,761 books by 357 authors.

Although anybody can read the books, only registered users can download complete books by selecting the "Download Complete Book" link in the Toolbox bar on table of contents pages – the first page you reach on selecting a title. Membership also allows you to mark a book as read and to annotate of the text. Annotations, if any, are also included when you retrieve a complete book. Registration is free, does not require personal information, and the FAQ notes "enables you to use other existing and future tools". The contents page also contains an 'Additional Book Info' box, with the date it was added to the collection, translator and edition information (if available), and the chance for registered users to add a rating for the book.

Each entire chapter is displayed as a scrollable page on the screen; navigation at top and bottom of the chapter allows direct access to the next chapter, or return to the previous chapter or the table of contents. Downloading the entire book simply creates a single HTML page containing all of the chapters, with a table of contents at the top, from which it is possible to link to chapters beginning further down the page. There is currently no possibility of other formats such as PDF.

91. **Roehampton University Children's Literature Collection**
   See also: **Froebel Archive Digital Collection**
   Children's literature
   http://core.roehampton.ac.uk/digital/chlitindex.htm

The Children's Literature Collection, housed in the Learning Resources Centre, exists to support children's literature studies at Roehampton University and the work of the National Centre for Research in Children's Literature (NCRCL). It includes reference books and journals, and many children's books of historical interest, mainly from the nineteenth and early twentieth centuries.

Eleven of these have now been digitised in their entirety, including the covers, frontispieces and any colour illustrations. The titles are: R.M. Ballantyne's *Black Ivory;* Brenda's Froggy's *Little Brother;* Maria Edgeworth's *Rosamond - A Series of Tales;* Henty's *With Clive in India;* L.T. Meade's *Scamp and I - A Story of City By-Ways;* Mrs Molesworth's *Sheila's Mystery;* Mary Sherwood's *The History of the Fairchild Family;* Catherine Sinclair's *Holiday House;* two editions (the second in colour) of Hesba Stretton's *Jessica's First Prayer* and Charlotte Yonge's *Countess Kate.*

As with the Froebel Archive Digital Collection, the author/title list leads to an extended contents page giving access to four-page PDF sections.

92.   Shakespeare Quartos Archive
See also: **William Shakespeare, The Complete Works of; William Shakespeare's Library** and **The Works of the Bard**. The 1914 Oxford editions of the *Complete Works of William Shakespeare,* said to rank among the most authoritative published in the century, can be found in **Bartleby** (*see*).
Literature
http://www.quartos.org/

The Shakespeare Quartos Archive is a digital collection of pre-1642 editions of William Shakespeare's plays. The cross-Atlantic collaboration (the Joint Information Systems Committee – JISC in the UK and the National Endowment for the Humanities in the USA) has also produced an interactive interface for detailed study, with full functionality for all thirty-two quarto copies of Hamlet (cover-to-cover digital reproductions and transcriptions) held by participating institutions. The software allows viewing the quartos separately or in parallel with any number of copies, and searching and annotation, as well as the creation of exhibits or character cue line lists, downloading and printing of both text and images. Eventually there will be at least one copy of every edition of William Shakespeare's plays printed in quarto before the theatres closed in 1642.

Individual copies can be viewed from the home page as images, HTML or XML, or the XML file can be downloaded.

If you enter the archive, you can select an edition, which will then open in a viewer which allows magnification/zooming and changes to the opacity of the image. It is also possible to view the text from the page and to make notes (if you are logged in).

93.   Shareware eBook.com
Literature
http://www.sharewareebooks.com/

Linked with e-book vendor eBooks.com (http://www.ebook.com/), Shareware eBooks.com allows you to view part of an e-book free of charge prior to purchasing the full title. Rare completely free e-books may be located but there is no mechanism to isolate these. The home page presents a series of cover images in three columns: Editor's Choice, Featured, and Multimedia, as well as the ability to select by sub-category and/or language and search by keyword; there is also a link to an advanced search that includes the ability to locate e-books about specified geographical locations. "Top 10 Last Week" (downloads? sales?) and categories are listed in a left-hand column.

Selecting an e-book takes users to a screen with information about the publisher, ISBN, the date uploaded and number of downloads, file size (often given as zero) and limitations (e.g. "1 Free Chapter. $24.99 to buy"); beneath this are four tabs: "Publisher's description", "Editor's review", "User reviews", and "Your review" and buttons for "View in Browser" and "Download Standalone". There is a note to the effect that in order to view the standalone version, the installation of the small DNL Reader is required; at the time of this review the same was true for "View in Browser" (both Firefox 3.0 and Internet Explorer).

94.   Smithsonian Institution Digital Library
Various
http://www.sil.si.edu/DigitalCollections/browse_BHL.cfm

While many of the titles included here are available within the Biodiversity Heritage Library (*see*) some are not – all are listed on the Digital Collections page. The search function at the head of the page searches across all digital library projects and may thus locate items other than two dozen e-books listed.

The titles clearly indicated as Biodiversity Heritage Library, open to a standard volume 'home page' with bibliographical and access details. Access may include 'View text' (which confusingly offers page facsimiles), uncorrected OCR text, and PDF (either Internet Archive (*see*) or Smithsonian Libraries). Non Biodiversity titles open at non-standard volume (or series) home pages offering varied access to the contents.

Navigation for facsimile pages varies but will at least offer immediate access to previous and next pages as well as to a requested page. It appears that all pages open at a magnification to fit the screen width, so that scrolling, or a change of magnification, is required to see the whole page.

95.   Spineless Books
Fiction / Poetry
http://www.spinelessbooks.com/

This unusual site with its minimalist front page gives access to books for which a charge is made as well as e-books in a variety of formats (HTML, PDF, MP3, Flash, CGI) some of which are free while others only offer excerpts. There are only four links from the foot of the home page (order, read, write and qu'est-ce que c'est que ca?) and a search box labeled "cross-reference by lexical item". Founded in Illinois in 2002, Spineless Books is "an independent publishing house dedicated to the production and distribution of printed and electronic literature, with an emphasis on collaborative writing, formal experimentation, artists' books, and utopian thought."

The 'read' link takes users to tabular page with an initial column with the cover image as well as columns headed: title, who, what, year, print, electronic, url, and interactivity. These are filled in variously for each title/row and lead to different iterations and versions. Not all have electronic counterparts. Some further texts can be found by following the 'write' link which leads to the 'Literature Laboratory'.

96.   Textbook Media
Textbooks
http://www.textbookmedia.com/

Not all books on the site are free. Low-cost paperbacks are available for most titles and are shipped directly to you.

It is necessary for both students and instructors to register before selecting a textbook and version from the booklist. Books are placed in your shopping cart for checking out. Even if you have selected a free product, it is necessary to go through the checkout process in order to activate the order.

Books can be browsed by subject, author or title or the catalogue can be searched. Pricing information is offered for each title – often offering a low-cost sponsored PDF, a PDF without advertisements, a print plus online bundle or an iPhone version.

All online versions require *Silverlight™*, free downloadable software from Microsoft.

The end-user license agreement states specifically that "any reproduction, retransmission, or republication of all or part of any of **The Content** found on our Site – including any and all downloaded content – is expressly prohibited, unless TM has specifically granted its prior written consent to so reproduce, retransmit, or republish **The Content**."

97.   Universal Digital Library
Various
http://www.ulib.org/
http://www.dcd.zju.edu.cn/ULIB2 (China, South)

Sub-headed **The Million Book Collection**, with a vision to provide a "universal digital library, widely available through free access on the Internet, [which] will improve the global society in ways beyond measurement," the Universal Digital Library aims to "foster creativity and free access to all human knowledge". While it is understood that the primary long-term objective to capture all books in digital format could take hundreds of years and never be completed, "a first step was to demonstrate the feasibility by undertaking to digitize 1 million books (less than 1% of all books in all languages ever published). This was achieved in the 2006 - 2007 timeframe." The project continues to digitise books at 50 scanning centers around the world in order to achieve the long term objective. The latest statistics given on the web site (by subject, language and year) are for the end of November 2007, at which point 119,894 books had been digitised; the home page shows copyright as 2001-2008.

It is possible to browse the archive by author, title, century /decade, subject or language lists. Advanced search allows author or title keywords in any language, and selection of subject, language, country as a range of years, and like the simple search results in a window to the left of the screen listing titles with author, language, year of publication, a subject term and the total number of pages, with an empty window to the right with the instruction "*Click on book title to view more details about it"* – more complete bibliographic data with a table of contents (if available) is then provided; some books are noted as unavailable (in full). Clicking on the "Read online [format e.g. HTML or TIFF]" opens a reader in a new window or tab. The reader software has limited functionality and only shows "n of xx pages" with buttons to move forward/backwards by one page or to the first or last available pages. A drop-down menu appears to offer the visible page in other formats (e.g. plain text – TXT) but this function did not work on any of the books viewed and it is more likely that it merely reflects the format of the book being viewed. Clicking the viewer for some of the more recent books opened a 3rd-party, remote site with the document view (e.g. the Food and Agriculture Organization of the United Nations).

It should be noted that identical simple searches on the Internet Archive limited to Universal Library, and in the Universal Digital Library do not give identical results. In all cases the Internet Archive search returns many fewer hits.

98.   Universal Library
Various
http://www.archive.org/details/universallibrary

The Universal Library Project, or the Universal Digital Library (*see*), also known as the **Million Books Project/Collection** and contained within the Internet Archive (*see*), was pioneered by Jaime Carbonell, Raj Reddy, Michael Shamos, Gloriana St Clair, and Robert Thibadeau of Carnegie Mellon University. The Internet Archive's introduction to the collection notes that the "Governments of India, China, and Egypt are helping fund this effort through scanning facilities and personnel. The Internet Archive has contributed 100k books from the Kansas City Public Library along with servers to India. The Indian government scanned the appropriate books. The Internet Archive has performed automated conversion of these scans into this collection." Sub-collections are the Million Book Project, which was an early collection of books from the Indian scanning centers of the Universal Library Project (many of these books are not complete or in good shape); The China-US Million Book Digital Library Project comprising books from the China-US Million Book Digital Library Project (CADAL); and books from Zhejiang University Library.

Within the Internet Archive, access is by a simple search (restricted to Universal Library') at the top of the home page or by an advanced search feature, which allows combinations of up to 11 terms, dates, collections, etc. When a title is selected from the search results, a page is returned containing a bibliographic record (including copyright status) with additional selected metadata and reviews (if any have been added), as well as the formats in which it may be downloaded. Normally these include: Read Online, PDF, ePub, Kindle, Daisy, full text, and DjVu. As with BookServer, PDF versions are scrollable files of facsimile pages, which may be printed or have images and/or text copied-and-pasted. There is also a search-within-text function.

It should be noted that identical simple searches on the Internet Archive limited to Universal Library, and in the Universal Digital Library do not give identical results. In all cases the Internet Archive search returns many fewer hits.

99. University of Virginia Electronic Texts Centre
Various humanities
http://etext.lib.virginia.edu/collections/subjects/

A number of the collections shown on this page are available only to University of Virginia staff and students. However, The Modern English Collection (AD 1500-present); most of The Middle English Collection; Shakespeare Resources; Religious Resources; The Dictionary of the History of Ideas; Special Collections electronic texts; British Poetry 1780-1910: a Hypertext Archive; and many other individual works can be accessed freely.

Entering a collection such as the Modern English Collection allows users to browse by the author's last name and ten select a title edition. This may take you directly to an illustrated poem or to the text by way of a contents page, which links to individual chapter and sections as well as to a complete text. Selecting a chapter produces a long HTML page with original pagination shown. Illustrations are placed as in the original, and link to larger copies.

100. Victorian Prose Archive
Literature
http://www.victorianprose.org/

This is a collection of Victorian Texts of Scholarly Interest maintained by Alfred J. Drake, PhD, University of California, Irvine. To date there are works by Matthew Arnold (*Culture and*

Anarchy, On Translating Homer...); Thomas Carlyle (*Past and Present*); James Anthony Froude (*English in the West Indies,* Ch. 5); Francis W. Newman (*Homeric Translation in Theory and Practice*); Cardinal Newman (*Discourses on ... University Education*); Walter Horatio Pater (*Complete Works,* with earlier editions); J.J. Thomas (*Froudacity*) and Oscar Wilde (*Dorian Gray, Intentions* in early versions).

On each author's page, there is a list of titles with links to the PDF file and a note of the file size and publication details for the edition. Some texts are also available as HTML and these, apart from the shorter ones are available as ZIP files.

101. Wikibooks
Textbooks
http://en.wikibooks.org/wiki/Main_Page

Wikibooks describes itself as "a Wikimedia community for creating a free library of educational textbooks that anyone can edit" – some 36,000 content pages in all. Only instructional books are included: textbooks, annotated texts, instructional guides, and manuals. The complete library is built using the wiki so textbooks (or textbook pages) can be added, edited and cross-linked by readers as well as original authors (interestingly – unlike Wikipedia – there is no requirement to have an account in order to edit; if you do not your changes are recorded against an IP address). Readers may consider that this is reason enough to stay clear of Wikibooks, but the idea that textbook authors are likely to keep an eye on their pages and remove mischievous changes may act as some reassurance. The chief concern for readers may be that most textbooks do not have any readily available attribution – even some of the featured books only have a statement such as "Students in ME 513: Engineering Acoustics started this Wikibook, *Engineering Acoustics*, during the fall semester 2005. Some pages of this book contain author credits." All content on Wikibooks is available for use under the both Creative Commons Attribution/Share-Alike License 3.0 and GNU Free Documentation License in order to ensure that books remain freely distributable forever.

Textbooks are grouped by subject with four top-level domains: Natural Sciences; Social Sciences, Computing and Humanities. There is also a 'Special Groups' category, which includes *Cookbook* and *Wikijunior* – both the subject of separate entries in this directory. Also available from the Wiki's main page are:

featured books (these tend to me more substantial and possibly better formatted), a comprehensive help and information section, a browsing page (by subject, Dewey or Library of Congress Classification, category, title, and audience. Moving to any of the subject pages brings readers to a page with space for listings of titles, featured books, related subjects, PDF books, print-ready books and 'Books with Public Collections' (of teaching materials, etc).

Textbooks may be single-page wiki entries or formed of separate pages (e.g. for each chapter), or – in some cases – only available as PDF downloads; others have separate printable and/or PDF versions available. Most textbooks follow the familiar wiki format, beginning with a list of sections (and sometimes sub-sections) which can be used for quick access; content pages are then divided into usually short sections of text. All pages retain the normal wiki navigation on the left-hand side. Although most pages begin with an image beside the content block, illustrations are generally sparse and content textual.

102.   **William Shakespeare, The Complete Works of**
        See also: **The Works of the Bard; William Shakespeare's Library** and **Shakespeare Quartos Archive**. The 1914 Oxford editions of the *Complete Works of William Shakespeare,* said to rank among the most authoritative published in the century, can be found in **Bartleby** (*see*).
        Literature
        http://the-tech.mit.edu/Shakespeare/

One of the earliest collections of e-books, this Massachusetts Institute of Technology site had been making available Shakespeare's plays and poetry since 1993. It claims to be the Web's first edition of the Complete Works of William Shakespeare, and offers a very simple site with a homepage listing what is available as comedy, history, tragedy and poetry. Clicking on the title of any play produces a top-level page listing all Acts and Scenes for separate access as well as links to the "Entire play in one page" and the Arden edition at Amazon. In turn, each scene has links to the previous and next scenes, to the play's top page and to the web site's homepage. The four poems (*A Lover's Complaint, The Rape of Lucrece, Venus and Adonis, Funeral Elegy by W.S.*) are accessed directly from the homepage, while *The Sonnets* have an intermediate page listing tem individually.

The plays are presented without a list of 'Persons Represented' or *Dramatis Personae* and with the text indented under each speaker's full name, with stage directions italicised. As both of the Shakespeare site mentioned here are based on the same print edition, in the interest of fairness the following note appears here and in the description for The Works of the Bard (*see*).

Additional line indentations and broken lines are not shown, and the text – listed only as from 'the Complete Moby(tm) Shakespeare' – is based on The Stratford Town modern-spelling edition of 1911, edited by Arthur Bullen and originally made available on the Internet by Grady Ward. Thus, the Moby Shakespeare is derived from a text that is said to "contain inaccuracies and unconventional pointing" (*CEAMagazine* 2000: 3-14). An example can be seen when the scroll from the gold casket is read by Morocco in Act II, Scene vii of *The Merchant of Venice,* which begins here as:

> All that glitters is not gold;
> Often have you heard that told:

rather than:

> All that glisters is not gold—
> Often have you heard that told;

103. William Shakespeare's Library
See also: **The Works of the Bard; The Complete Works of William Shakespeare** and **Shakespeare Quartos Archive**. The 1914 Oxford editions of the *Complete Works of William Shakespeare,* said to rank among the most authoritative published in the century, can be found in **Bartleby** (*see*).
Literature
http://www.yudu.com/library/45988/William-
   Shakespeare--s-Library

Yudu, best known for the online publication and self-publishing of digital magazines, produced – in time for Shakespeare's 2010 birthday, William Shakespeare's Library, which they describe as "a complete collection of William Shakespeare's works" with 45 titles, including *A Lover's Complaint; Funeral Elegy; The Passionate Pilgrim* (an anthology of poems attributed to Shakespeare); *The Phoenix and the Turtle; The Rape of Lucrece; The Sonnets;* and *Venus and Adonis*. There is no information on the site about the edition from which these versions are derived, but it is interesting to note that the word "glisters" (*see* Works of the Bard and Complete Works) is here correctly used so we can deduce that these are not The Moby Shakespeare editions.

Hovering over a cover in the library bookshelves reveals the beginning of the brief publisher's description of the work that can be read in full on the subsequent page, which also offers the facility to embed the work in your own web site and to view the work. After a brief pause while the work is loaded in Adobe Flash, a facsimile book is presented. Having entered a book, there is no clear way (other than the browser's back button) to return to the library. On a page facing the front cover is a link to instructions for use, and along the top of the screen are a number of tools; page turning is induced – with a slight rustle of paper – by clicking on the lower corner of each page. The available tools include the possibility to move to next/previous, first/last or any numbered page as well as print (with a choice of page range), bookmark in several colours, add notes or highlights to the current page and change to a "plain text" (i.e. in HTML rather than the facsimile) version. Pages can be magnified or set to fill the existing screen width and there are menus allowing readers to share the book (e.g. Del.icio.us), view thumbnails of all pages in a left-hand column or of only those pages with highlighting/notes, and of options which include downloading an offline version, setting preferences, viewing in single-page mode, and auto-presenting with a page-turn at designated intervals.

The text is clearly set out on the page – although it is not entirely without fault, as shown for example, by an unnecessary line break resulting in a stage instruction that extends to two single-word lines in *Anthony and Cleopatra*, as well as by punctuation and line indentations that do not correspond with other, scholarly editions.

104. **The Works of the Bard**
See also: **The Complete Works of William Shakespeare; William Shakespeare's Library** and **Shakespeare Quartos Archive.** The 1914 Oxford editions of the *Complete Works of William Shakespeare,* said to rank among the most authoritative published in the century, can be found in **Bartleby** (*see*).
Literature
http://www.it.usyd.edu.au/~matty/Shakespeare/

Noting pedantically that "this site is the web's first edition of Shakespeare. The text is based on the same text as the MIT site but came online in October 1993, two months before the MIT site" (*see* The Complete Works...), the site offers the same minimally-formatted text of Shakespeare's plays. It contains the same plays from the same source – The Moby Shakespeare – as the MIT site but contains two additional poems – *The Passionate Pilgrim* and *The Phoenix and The Turtle*, while lacking the *Funeral Elegy*. Although the source is the same, this site includes the *Dramatis Personae* for each play. Again the complete play can be accessed as a single web page in addition to the individual scenes, but here a plain-text version is also available. In the interest of fairness the following note also appears in the MIT description.

Additional line indentations and broken lines are not shown, and the text – listed only as from 'the Complete Moby(tm) Shakespeare which is freely available online' – is based on The Stratford Town modern-spelling edition of 1911, edited by Arthur Bullen and originally made available on the Internet by Grady Ward. Thus, the Moby Shakespeare is derived from a text that is said to "contain inaccuracies and unconventional pointing" (*CEAMagazine* 2000: 3-14). An example can be seen when the scroll from the gold casket is read by Morocco in Act II, Scene vii of *The Merchant of Venice,* which begins here as:
> All that glitters is not gold;
> Often have you heard that told:
rather than:
> All that glisters is not gold—
> Often have you heard that told;

World eBook Library *see* **World Public Library**

105. World Public Library

Various

http://www.netlibrary.net/index.htm

Also known as **World eBook Library**, found at a mirror site, http://worldebooklibrary.org/index.htm.

The home page is misleadingly entitled in the browser: "World Public Library Association".

Since first visited, the World eBook Library has become a member-only subscription resource and consequently no longer offers any free e-books in its 125 collections totaling some 750,000 PDF e-books. Interestingly these collections include some that offer their material freely from their own web sites, such as the Alex Catalogue of Electronic Texts (*see*) and ETANA: Electronic Tools and Ancient Near Eastern Archives (*see*).

106. WOWIO

Various

http://www.wowio.com/wowiobooks

On the main WOWIO site, authors set their own prices, and keep all of the income less the credit card processing fee of those prices. WOWIO also has proprietary technology that allows e-books to be sponsored, making them free to readers. Advertisers subsidise or buy the book for the reader, and the reader tells their friends. As those friends download the free e-book the advertisers expand their reach with more one-to-one relationships with consumers. In the ../wowiobooks part of the site, e-books are free or near-free ($0.99).

The home page features six to eight e-books – some with brief descriptions – that can be read online or downloaded as PDF files. The home page can also be changed by users to show books by genre or by series. The search and browse boxes at the top of the page, however, appear to revert to searching across the whole site and mix free, near-free and charged books in the results.

Once a choice of book is made, a book description page is supplied with information on the number of pages and the size of the download file, the 'ISBN' (which is the format 'WOWIO-00552') and titles which readers of this book have also viewed. A short description is followed by links to recommend the book, similar books by category, and links that can be placed on your site either to the book on WOWIO or to WOWIO itself. Typically, books can be freely read online or downloaded/sent as a gift in PDF for the near-free price.

Reading online opens a new browser with facsimile-reading software showing a page image of the cover. Free books are copyrighted to WOWIO and state specifically that no part of the book may be reproduced in any form without written permission of the copyright owner. It also notes that the information in the book is "furnished for information use only, is subject to change without notice, and should not be construed as a comment by WOWIO LLC. WOWIO LLC assumes no responsibility for any errors or inaccuracies that may appear in this book." The reader software allows single or double page shift left and double page shift right views – effectively shift left shows facing pages while shift right shows the front and back of a single page adjacent to each other on the screen. There are also two levels of magnification, the ability to bookmark, to download the PDF from within the book, and an information button which shows the information from the book description page. Page turning buttons are also in the tool bar at the top of the pages.

107. Yale: Harvey Cushing/John Hay Whitney Medical Historical Library
Classical medicine
http://www.med.yale.edu/library/find/digital.html

When first examined in mid-2010, the Historical Library, in collaboration of Richard H. Siderits of the Robert Wood Johnson University Hospital at Hamilton, New Jersey, was making available electronic versions of several popular medical texts from the 15th to the 18th centuries. At that time about thirteen texts were available and these were listed on a home page. Brief bibliographic details were given for each title. This led to a fuller descriptive page, which included access to the contents by chapter or groups of pages. In some cases, the sections linked to a page of thumbnail page images from which a start page could be chosen. In other instances the link was to an HTML page containing all the pages of the section. Disappointingly this was the case for Nicholas Culpeper's *The English physitian: or an astrologo-physical discourse of the vulgar herbs of this nation*.

Revisited in January 2011, only nine 'Books By and About Harvey Cushing' appear to be available (not including the Culpeper) from the new web address given above. In each case the book is available as an HTML page view or as a 'simulated book' with tools to zoom, move the book on the screen, scribble, take notes, etc. *From a Surgeon's Journal 1915-1918* contains some terribly sad descriptions of field surgery during the Passchendaele battles.

Then, as with the current site, facsimile images open with only navigation within the book, so that to move to other titles it is necessary to user the browser's Back button.

PUBLISHERS
Mainstream Publishers

108.   Badosa
         Novels, short stories, poetry
         http://www.badosa.com/

Badosa publishes in English, Castilian, Catalan and French, and the e-books on the site include: some 320 short stories, 29 novels and 1,386 poems by 191 authors. The home page offers immediate details of a few titles and, on the left, links to the short stories, poetry and novels as well as to Worldwide Classics and – slightly oddly – to a separate Ebooks page, where access is by language (English and French are together), and where there is a note to the effect that downloaded e-books are in the right format for Microsoft Reader and for the iPhone / iPad Touch using the Stanza reader. The site is lightly supported by 'Ads by Google'.

To the left of the home page, beneath the links to short stories, etc are links to lists of authors and the most popular titles, and to 'My Bookshelf', 'Excerpta' – a search facility, and to 'Map of fictions' where the origin of each title is plotted on a world map using coloured flags to denote the four different languages.

Each selection of titles is shown as a scrollable list of detailed records; each record begins with a grey title box showing the title, author, genre, number of words, language, the name of the collection (e.g. Global Fiction) and the date of publication. Beneath this is a row of icons enabling users to read or download the book (not all titles can be downloaded), add the title to a personal bookshelf, comment, and create a 'permalink' to the title. Beneath this again is a brief description followed by the first few lines of the text.

A selection from this list will take readers directly to the first page of the first chapter as a scrollable HTML page. The icons for adding to a personal bookshelf, sharing opinions and creating a permalink are joined by two more: changing the text size and a direct link to the map – but here, a large-scale map showing the source of the title in question. In some cases there is also an icon linking to the e-book page: a summary page with a table of contents, information about the author. At the foot of the page are links to next and previous pages (with some indication of progress: 7/79) and a summary table of metadata with information on copyright, works by the same author, date of publication, collection and permalink. Finally, there are readers' opinions/reviews.

109.   Cliffs Notes
Textbooks
http://www.cliffsnotes.com/

While some of the CliffsNotes titles are available in aggregations such as NetLibrary, ALL titles in the series are freely available from the John Wiley/CliffsNotes web site. The CliffsNotes Study Guides originally covered only literature, but many hundreds of articles ("homework help") – some with CliffsNotes titles available – are now available on the web site for Algebra, Basic Mathematics, Biology, Calculus, Chemistry, Economics, Geometry, History, Physics, Psychology, Spanish, and Writing. All of the Literature CliffsNotes titles are available, and access to these is offered by Books & Novels, Drama & Plays, Philosophy & Essays, Poetry, Shakespeare, and Short Stories, as well as via an alphabetic title list.

Each book page begins with a short summary, which is followed by a detailed table of contents offering access to individual parts and chapters. Each is published as an HTML page. Within the literature series, analysis of the original title (novel, play, etc) is normally by chapter or act / scene – these are offered as HTML pages with a series of tabs, usually: Summary, Analysis, Read the original text, and Glossary at the top.

The site is supported by advertising, which can be distracting. Citation help is provided for both the articles and the CliffsNotes titles. CliffsNotes® To Go Literature reviews are also available for the iPhone & iPod touch.

110.   Shearsman Books
Poetry
http://www.shearsman.com/pages/books/ebooks/ebooks
_home.html

Since 2003, Shearsman Books has published volumes of poetry through print-on-demand – they describe themselves as a "very active publisher of new poetry, mostly from Britain and the USA, but also with an active translation list"; now, in addition, some e-books are available for free download from their site. Currently nineteen titles can be downloaded, and more are promised. Titles are listed on the single e-books page, and for each title there is a cover image, a brief description, a file size, pagination, and the e-publication date. Each volume downloads into a single scrollable PDF page.

111.   Tor.com
Science Fiction/Fantasy
http://www.tor.com/index.php?option=com_content&view
=stories

A small selection of science fiction and fantasy novellas and short stories in either graphic or weblog format is available from this page of a much larger web site devoted to the genre. The stories written in blogs may be single long pages or may extend over a number of individual 'chapter' pages. Many of the illustrations which head the blogs or make up the graphic novels are exceptionally well executed. As the site is structured around a blog, in each format, pages conclude with readers' comments.

112.   Volramos
Various
http://www.volramos.co.uk/volramos_ebooks.html

** Site reported as unavailable January 2011 **

Volramos Digital Publishing has a few e-books available at prices between £1.99 and £6.00 as well as some free on this e-books page and a separate free e-books page with a further three e-books. Free titles include *5 Tips to Amazing Legs, Doorways of Malta, Photoshop Takeway* and *Max Your Metabolism, Part 1.* Several further titles are promised.

University Presses

113.   Columbia University Press: gutenberg<e>
Monographs (History)
http://www.gutenberg-e.org/

Funded by the Andrew W. Mellon Foundation, the Gutenberg-e prize comes from a collaboration between Columbia University Press and the American Historical Association, with the aim of exploring and promoting the electronic publication of scholarly writing. Thus, the titles in the collection "represent the most distinguished and innovative scholarship delivered with creative and thoughtful use of digital technology." All have been rigorously peer-reviewed. There is no connection with Project Gutenberg (*see*).

Some 35 titles are directly accessible from the home page, covering a range of topics including Africa, colonial Latin America, South Asia, Europe before 1800, Military history and history of foreign relations, History of North America before 1900, and Women's History or History of Gender; there is also a search (but no browse) facility. It is not possible to discover the extent of the collection.

Books are presented with an initial illustrated 'cover' beside a table of contents, from which individual chapters or sections can be selected. Each chapter is presented as a single, scrollable HTML page with a static title header across the top of the page and pagination indicated in the right-hand margin. Where chapters are subdivided into sections, there is a linked list of sections at the head of each chapter.

114.   digitalculturebooks
Monographs and textbooks
http://www.digitalculture.org/

A publishing venture of the University of Michigan Press and the Scholarly Publishing Office of the University of Michigan Library which is creating a list of titles that are available for free online and for sale in print. The imprint is dedicated to publishing innovative work in new media studies and the emerging field of digital humanities: that is, all aspects of new media and its impact on society, culture, and scholarly communication. The web site notes that the "imprint aspires to both investigate and demonstrate new forms of scholarly practice in the humanities."

digitalculturebooks is also an experimental publishing strategy with a strong research component. As the titles are available both in print and online, digitalculturebooks hopes "to:

- develop an open and participatory publishing model that adheres to the highest scholarly standards of review and documentation;
- develop a model for press/library collaboration at Michigan and elsewhere;
- showcase and extend Michigan's leading role in the development of digital resources;
- encourage and participate in a national dialogue about the future of scholarly communication."

At the time of writing, fourteen titles are available.

115. Dumbarton Oaks Research Library
Monographs
http://www.doaks.org/publications/doaks_online_publicati
ons.html

Dumbarton Oaks publishes in three subject areas: Byzantine Studies; Garden and Landscape Studies; and Pre-Columbian Studies. Some texts are made available on the web in an effort to increase access to the material. Single copies may be printed for individual use. The open access titles in all three areas are directly available from the home page; there is also a search option. All books are also available (at cost) from Harvard University Press.

A selected title first shows the hard-copy cover and an extended abstract or description of the work, followed by the print version's ISBN/publication data. There is also a link above the abstract to the 'contents and electronic texts'. Following this link produces a chapter list with a note of the print cost. The full text and illustrations of each chapter are accessed with Acrobat Reader so that texts, captions, and footnotes are fully searchable using the software's find option.

116. ELT Press: University of North Carolina Greensboro English Department
English Literature in Translation 1880-1920
http://www.eltpress.org/ebooks.html

Only four e-books seem to be available: George H. Thomson's *Dorothy Richardson: A Calendar of Letters; Hogan, M.P.* which is a three-volume novel by May Laffan Hartley; *The Editions of Dorothy Richardson's 'Pilgrimage': A Comparison of Texts* by George H. Thomson and Dorothy F. Thomson; and *Pater in the 1990s* edited by Laurel Brake & Ian Small.

In each case, an initial contents page leads to PDF chapter files.

117.   GAIA: Global, Area and International Archive (University of California)
Scholarly
http://repositories.cdlib.org/gaia/gaia_books/

GAIA is a collaboration between International and Area Studies at the University of California, Berkeley, the University of California Press, the California Digital Library, and research units on other University of California campuses. GAIA is a peer-reviewed initiative within the eScholarship Digital Repository. All GAIA volumes are published digitally and made available free of charge to a global network of scholars. The goal "is to publish the best peer-reviewed scholarship within both established area and regional studies and new areas of inquiry that break down boundaries between traditional disciplines and regions." GAIA publishes English-language manuscripts from scholars throughout the world and occasionally also republishes out-of-print "classics" in global and international studies. At the time of review there were 214 publications in this collection, published between 1995 and 2010, of which 58 are e-books.

An author/title list can be browsed and an individual work selected. At this point the screen is divided, with a narrower column to the left containing bibliographic details, a 'Search Document' function and a list of 'Similar Items'. The main body of the page contains facsimile pages which may be scrolled or navigated by moving to previous/next, first/last or a numbered page; only approximately half a page is visible at a time with conventional browser settings. As is normal with this type of display the virtual page number does not relate to the book pagination. Also across the top of the screen are links to the abstract, e-mail, share (Twitter, Facebook, etc), cite (one citation style only), save (to 'My Items' – link at top of page) and purchase (the hard copy).

118. National Defence University (Institute for National Strategic Studies)
Monographs
http://www.ndu.edu/inss/index.cfm?pageID=8&type=page

The Institute for National Strategic Studies (INSS) produces reports and "numerous publications written by subject matter experts for decision makers at all levels of the Department of Defense, government and the community at large" and this site features a 'Publications' page, which lists items under Centre for Strategic Research; Centre for Complex Operations; Centre for Technology and National Strategic Policy; and INSS. Many, if not all, of these titles are freely available as PDF files. Publications dating from before 2009 can be found in three areas of the digital library linked from the publications page.

119. Ohio State University Press
Various (mostly literature)
http://www.ohiostatepress.org/index.htm?/books/openaccess.htm

Ohio State University Press describes its mission as "to disseminate the best scholarship as widely as possible." Accordingly, the complete texts of around 90 books are available in PDF from the web site – these appear to be titles no longer in print. The Press also notes that "all titles available this way, whether old or new, have gone through the exact same peer review process as our printed books. Any book that carries our imprint – no matter what medium is being used – has been approved by our Editorial Board after a thorough vetting process." The books may only be used for personal study, remain as copyright of the author or publisher and may not be used for commercial purposes.

The available titles are listed by author on the open access home page (this URL) and there is no means of searching or browsing by subject. Each title is accessed via a page containing its table of contents which in turn links to PDF files of the chapters. The top-level book page also contains the note: "Open access is better with open dialogue. Click here to leave or read comments and critiques about this book". Chapters open in a new tab or browser window so that access to subsequent chapters is easily effected by the original table of contents.

120. Penn State Romance Studies
Scholarly
http://dpubs.libraries.psu.edu/DPubS?Service=UI&versio
n=1.0&verb=Display&handle=psu.rs

Essentially, a peer-reviewed monograph series, Romance Studies is also an open access experiment. The terms of use note that it "gives readers the options to view the content freely online and to purchase a print edition. Allowing free access promotes engagement with scholarship." It goes on to say that "Though this material is provided freely, policies regarding your use of Romance Studies are still governed by copyright laws. Romance Studies materials should be used for non-commercial, educational, and research purposes."

Currently there are just four titles available. Each contents page offers PDF files for each chapter and a search within the book facility. The titles are: Juliette Rogers' *Career Stories: Belle Époque Novels of Professional Development*; Dorothy Kelly's *Reconstructing Woman: From Fiction to Reality in the Nineteenth-Century French Novel*; Sarah H Beckjord's *Territories of History: Humanism, Rhetoric, and the Historical Imagination in the Early Chronicles of Spanish America*; and the edited work, *The Book of Peace - Christine de Pizan*, edited by Karen Green, Constant J. Mews, and Janice Pindar.

121. Project Euclid
Mathematical monographs and conference proceedings
http://projecteuclid.org/DPubS?Service=UI&version=1.0&
verb=Display&handle=euclid

Project Euclid aims to advance scholarly communication in the field of theoretical and applied mathematics and statistics. In part this is achieved through bringing together relevant journals and publications in the project web site. Many are available free of charge. Project Euclid was developed and made available by the Cornell University Library and is jointly managed by Cornell and the Duke University Press.

In addition to journals, the project has made six monograph series and one volume of conference proceedings (the Berkeley Symposium on Mathematical Statistics and Probability) available through open access – some 160 titles in all. There is a separate 'home page' for each of the six series from which the text may be searched or the series contents listed by individual title. Selecting a title produces a bibliographic record with an abstract, followed by a list of chapters, each with links to a chapter abstract and its PDF file.

Rotunda *see* **University of Virginia Press**

122.   University of Arizona Press
Various
http://www.uapress.arizona.edu/onlinebks/index.php

Around a dozen 'online books' are available from the home page of this site. These "are free for reading while you are visiting our web site, but are not free for download or distribution." Topics range from a guide to Arizonan weeds by way of the Hohokam Indians and *Women in Levi's* to near-earth space. The search facility at the head of the page searches the entire catalogue rather than the e-books list.

Books may be either HTML of PDF, but in every case the initial link from the home page takes readers to a table of contents/chapter list from which individual chapters can be accessed.

123.   University of California Press eScholarship Editions Public Titles
Scholarly
http://content.cdlib.org/search?sort=title&relation=eschol arship.cdlib.org&style=eschol&rights=Public

The Press has published around 2,000 of e-books – published between 1982 and 2004 – across all disciplines, including art, science, history, music, religion, and fiction, but only 770 are freely available as 'public access'. It is possible to search or browse by subject, title or author and then to limit the titles listed to those which are free. Results are presented (20 to the page) with a thumbnail cover image, publication details and three-lines of the publisher's description (which can be extended). Subject categories for each book are listed as links so that it is possible to move horizontally, and there is also a link to 'similar items'. The title link leads to a page divided vertically between a table of contents, and the publication details, cover image, and preferred citation. Once a chapter has been selected, the text – divided into pages equivalent to the print edition – is presented as a scrollable HTML file, again with the contents listed to the left.

124. University of Pittsburgh Press Digital Editions
Various
http://digital.library.pitt.edu/p/pittpress/

The University of Pittsburgh Press and the University Library System have worked in partnership to make some 590 books published by the Press available as e-books. The aim, in making them freely available on the Internet, is to enable greater access to the material previously available only as print editions. Titles are drawn from the Pitt Latin American Series, the Pitt Series in Russian and East European Studies, and Composition, Literacy and Culture. Most of these titles are currently out of print.

The list of titles may be browsed by author, subject or title, or searched. Results lists can be sorted by title or author, although the default display is unsorted. Each title in a results list is given with title, author and publication details, and links to the table of contents, 'View first page' or the possibility of adding to a 'bookbag' for later use. The table of contents is prefixed by a full bibliographic record with details of author, title, publication and series, availability, print source, subject terms and topic, and the full item URL. The table of contents lists the front cover, front matter, title page, index, etc as well as the individual chapters – all of which lead to facsimiles of the work.

Facsimile pages have simple previous and next links at the top and foot of each page and, by default, are generally are of a size to require scrolling to read the entire page. Summary bibliographic details and a print button also appear at the head of the page. The next link moves seamlessly from chapter to chapter, and the print button opens the facsimile page again without the surrounding navigational aids. Above the page-proper is a menu bar with links back to the search results, a note of the current page number, and the facility to both change the magnification and swap to a PDF file for the current page.

125. University of Virginia Press: Rotunda
Various
http://www.upress.virginia.edu/electronic_pubs.html

In the 1990s, the University of Virginia Press published two online reference works, *Afro-American Sources in Virginia* and the *Guide to African-American Documentary Resources in North Carolina* and these remain freely available at this URL. Also from this site, the Rotunda resource offers original scholarship and digitised critical and documentary editions (primary material such as letters, the papers of Thomas Jefferson or the American Constitution) in the humanities and social sciences. Free access to Rotunda is limited to a 48-hour free trial (longer access in order to perform a review or evaluate Rotunda for institutional purchase may be requested) and a user name and password are supplied by e-mail. Individuals are limited to one free trial per six-month period.

There are two Rotunda collections: The American Founding Era Collection (six subsets, plus The Dolley Madison Digital Edition – a stand-alone edition with special features) and The 19th-Century Literature and Culture Collection (also six subsets: Emily Dickinson, William Wells Brown, Herman Melville, Matthew Arnold, Christina Rossetti, and Emily Shore). The two collections must accessed and searched separately. It is necessary to 'drill down' through several levels of contents in each subset to reach a particular document, although searches take users directly into a document (search terms are highlighted). Documents are presented as paginated, scrollable text on the screen.

There is also a free online collection – Founders Early Access, which is not password protected. It makes available thousands of unpublished documents from America's founders: letters and other papers penned by famous figures such as James Madison, John Adams, George Washington and Thomas Jefferson.

126.   Wesleyan University Press
Monographs
http://www.wesleyan.edu/wespress/e-books/index.html

At the time of review only three volumes appear to be available: a volume on the Chinese sources and intertexts of Segalen's poetry: *Steles, Volume 2*; a work of regional history entitled *A History of The Eclectic Society of Phi Nu Theta, Volume 2* and a volume on science fiction: the *Wesleyan Anthology of Science Fiction Teacher's Guide*.

Each volume opens as a PDF file.

127.   Royal College of Pathologists
Reports
http://www.rcpath.org/index.asp?PageID=38

While this might not be seen as a collection of e-books, it is an example of professional body developing an freely accessible library of reports in a typical e-book format: PDF. The library is divided into the following sub-sets: General documents; Cancer datasets and tissue pathways; Clinical biochemistry; Cytopathology; Forensic pathology; Genetics; Haematology; Histocompatibility and immunogenetics; Histopathology; Immunology and allergy; Medical microbiology; Neuropathology; and Paediatric pathology. Some of the reports are quite lengthy and may also be purchased in hard copy; the majority are dated post-2000 while a few were originally published in the 1990s.

128.   Royal College of Surgeons of England
Reports / handbooks
http://www.rcseng.ac.uk/publications/docs

The Royal College of Surgeons notes that it "publishes the findings of its working parties and other groups established to study particular issues. Specific divisions of the College, such as the professional regulation division, publish documents relating to the regulations that apply to their activities and which are of importance to surgeons in training and those taking examinations." Perhaps between 12 and 18 reports or handbooks are published each year, and the entire library of titles going back to 1989 can be browsed by title, year or publisher (normally a sub-group of the College). Some of the older titles are only available from the library in print for a small charge but most are available as PDF files at no cost. Clicking on an individual title takes readers to a page with a facsimile of the cover, the title, date and publisher information and either the cost or a URL from which the file will download.